Bridging East & West

Kathie Wei-Sender

with Henry Jacobson

Title: Bridging East & West Kathie Wei-Sender
Author: Kathie Wei-Sender with Henry Jacobson
Library of Congress Control Number: 2022904478
ISBN 13: 979-8-9850707-2-9
First Edition
Editor: Meg Marsh
Designer: Bonnie Britt
Cover credit: Photo 15544008 / Moon Gate
© Sofiaworld | Dreamstime.com
United Press International photo of Deng Xiaoping and U.S. Presidents Jimmie Carter and Richard Nixon used by permission.
Publisher: Jade Falcon Publishers, Boca Raton, Fla.
Contact: Jadefalconpub@gmail.com

Dedication

To my children, who give me love and devotion; to my first husband, Chang-Jui, for giving me our three wonderful children; to my third husband, Henry, for giving me comfort and love in my later years; and to the memory of C.C. Wei, the love of my life, who gave me Precision.

Contents

Introduction

I **started** writing this book more than thirty years ago, soon after my first autobiography, *Second Daughter: Growing up in China, 1930-1949* was published in 1985. I returned home after an exhausting book tour (I was 55 at the time) and said to myself, "OK, Kathie, what now?" At the time I was still competing in international bridge competitions, helping to run a global shipping company, and meeting with American presidents to consult with them on Chinese-American diplomacy. I suppose I felt there was more of my story to tell.

Second Daughter (written with my co-author, Terry Quinn) explores my childhood and teen years in a China that no longer exists. I was part of a world of wealth and entitlement in an academic setting. Later, as circumstances changed in my country, I spent time in the ancestral birthplace of my father and was introduced to a feudal way of life. The communist takeover forced my family to reconsider our place in this new country, and with the help of my father I was able to leave for the United States. My family, however, did not have this option, and their ensuing travails are discussed in this memoir.

My father had the foresight—and the means—to arrange a new life for me, his second daughter. I took what he offered me and began my life in a country that afforded me safety, comfort, and no end of opportunity, of which I wholeheartedly took advantage. I was a nursing administrator for the

Triage and Trauma Emergency Center at Idlewild Airport for over 20 years, a CEO for a global shipping company, and a cultural liaison during the Reagan and Bush administrations, helping to foster warmer relations between the two world powers. But those who still recognize my name know me as Kathie Wei-Sender, the international bridge champion.

Bridge is not the popular game it was in the '40s and '50s, when, according to the Association of American Playing Card Manufacturers, the game was played in forty-four percent of American homes. Because of the COVID pandemic, face-to-face bridge clubs became more rare, yet the game has found a new resurgence on the Internet, where the website Bridge Base Online can host over 25,000 players at any given time, and over half a million in one day.

But the passion for bridge is difficult to explain to someone who thinks it is just a card game. David Owen, book reviewer for the *New Yorker,* wrote "One attraction [for bridge] is the sense of endlessly unfolding complexity: the more you learn, the less you feel you know." There are 635,013,559,600 possible bridge hands, and so many strategies for playing them. The experts can figure out what cards are in their opponents' hands in only a few plays, yet even a beginner with a few lessons under her belt can enjoy the satisfaction of playing a hand out well at the bridge table. As exhilarating as making (or defeating) a bridge contract can be, there are also times when even the most adept players feel humbled. The game is inexhaustible! My friend Henry wears a tee shirt that says it all: "If bridge is just a game, then the Grand Canyon is just a hole in the ground."

From China to the U.S.

Have regular hours for work and play;
make each day both useful and pleasant, and prove that you understand
the worth of time by employing it well.
Then youth will bring few regrets, and
life will become a beautiful success.
— Louisa May Alcott, *Little Women*

My bridge career has spanned nearly seventy years. I have won, along with my partners, four gold and four silver medals representing the United States in international bridge competition, and garnered national titles in nearly fifteen tournaments throughout the U.S. and North America. What has set me apart from my competitors has been the Precision Bidding System, a method created by my second husband and great love, Charles (C.C.) Wei. With Charles' guidance, I became Precision Bidding's promoter and advocate and with my talented partners, I attained stunning successes over the years using this method, currently used throughout the world by both amateur and expert bridge players. Who could have anticipated the opportunities a game of cards would afford me?

Through bridge, I have met and interacted with political leaders around the world. I've also had the chance to meet— and sometimes to play with— notable personalities including Warren Buffet, Sammy Davis, Jr., Malcolm Forbes, Omar Sharif, Burt Reynolds, and Oprah Winfrey.

However, a card game alone, no matter how splendid or challenging, does not identify me. Yes, in a way it *has* served as a 'bridge' to other opportunities in my life, and for this I am grateful. But now, confined by a global pandemic and the restrictions older age can bring, I find myself returning to the many events and people who accompanied me through my eventful life.

As I enter my tenth decade, my children offer me these words of encouragement: "Old age is a gift." When I reflect back on my life, I realize how true those words are. I've been blessed with a warm and loving family: three wonderful husbands, (whom I've sadly outlived), three great kids, and grand and great-grandchildren. I am grateful I can still enjoy all of my children at my age. My spirits are high, although I can't say I like being old.

Names

I was born in China in 1930—the Year of the Horse— as Yang Xiao-yen (Xiao pronounced 'shee-au'). 'Yang' was my last name (out of respect for the family, surname is given first); Xiao-yen, means 'little swallow.' My parents had four daughters, and each daughter's first name had two syllables, each with the same first syllable but a differing second. My sisters were Xiao-huei (Little Knowledge, or smart one), Xiao-ying, (Little Hero, or brave one) and Xiao-chin (Little Youth, or young one). Using the same first syllable in Chinese names is a common practice: this syllable is a 'generation' name by

which one can know immediately to which generation a child belongs. All children from a family with
the generation name, Xiao, for example, would have
the same mother and same father. This was especially important during a time when men were allowed
to have concubines. These 'girl friends' had children,
and it was necessary in Chinese society to be able
to distinguish between a man's concubine's children
and those of his legitimate wife.

My father had received two PhD degrees at
the University of Michigan before I was born, so he
was fluent in both English and his native Mandarin.
Because of his love for America and of the English
language, I learned to speak English at an early age.
My father gave me the English name Catherine.
My American friends ultimately shortened this to
"Kathie." When I married Shen Chang-Jui (pronounced shen jang ray), I changed the spelling of my
first name to Katherine, hoping to avoid the unwar-
ranted scrutiny of the government, which was in the
throes of Joseph McCarthy's Red Scare. McCarthy,
a junior senator from Wisconsin, was an aggresive
crusader against alleged communist subversion in
America.

After my divorce from Chang-Jui, I married
C.C. (Charles) Wei (pronounced 'way'). It was as
Kathie Wei that I began my bridge career. In 1987
Charles passed away, and six years later I married
Henry Sender, a Jewish man who was proud of
being both American and Jewish. When he asked
me to accept Judaism as my religion, I needed a

Hebrew name to use during the conversion ceremony. The first name suggested was *Tzipora*, which means 'bird' in Hebrew, and since my first name in Chinese means 'little swallow' I didn't want another 'bird' name. We ultimately agreed on the Hebrew name Rachel. Since I was already well known in the bridge world, it was important for my professional career that I retain the name 'Wei' but legally, I was now Kathie Wei-Sender. With all these changes of name, it's no wonder I need to search for my identity!

Early Childhood

I was born in Peking in 1930—now Beijing. My father taught at Yenching University in Peking, one of the most prestigious universities in China at the time. My formative years were spent among my parents' American friends, so it was natural that English would become my second language. English was spoken at home as well: Father had tremendous foresight and felt that the future lay in the U.S and not China. To that end, the Yang family was far more westernized than many of our contemporaries.

Father was dean of his department at the university, a position that granted our family much wealth and prestige. At their frequent dinner parties, one could recognize members of the Peking academic community, as well as dignitaries from Kuomintang, the Nationalist Party. My parents hosted these gatherings in a large, elaborately appointed parlor, decorated with Chinese paintings and calligraphy scrolls as well as Western prints. The dinner table was arranged with expertly folded linen napkins and silverware. Servants were always on hand to serve the finest delicacies. Distinguished guests could find a current selection of English novels and magazines stacked in the bookshelves, and big band music could be heard throughout the house. This was a home more adaptable to the comfort of Westerners than of Chinese—attributable in part to mother's collection of old *Better Homes and Gardens* magazines.

Mother could be the subject of her own book: in her own attempts to make her way in the *haute* society of intellectual elite China, she strove to present daughters who could impress her company with their virtuosity. As after-dinner entertainment, she would have my older sister Alice perform for the guests. Alice was a musical prodigy and could have played traditional Chinese melodies on the lute (accompanied by my grade-school folk dancing efforts) but mother would have none of that. Instead, she insisted Alice play "Jeepers, Creepers," a 1930s American jazz tune, with me dancing a crazy rendition of the Charleston, complete with arm-flailing and shimmy shaking. The image of two young Chinese children performing popular American song and dance standards provided a humorous, if somewhat incongruous image for our guests.

I must add here, that despite the fact that we performed according to our mother's wishes at these events, I was anything *but* the traditional, obedient

Chinese little girl. I remember how one day a friend of mother's came to visit. I hid in the leafy tree in our yard with my current weapon of preference—a slingshot. What an easy target from the vantage point of my lofty fortress. I didn't injure the friend, not seriously—but maybe my attack from above wasn't the most hospitable thing to do. My sisters and I all pointed fingers at each other, and I escaped any blame. But "obedient?" I don't think so!

Our home could have appeared somewhat strange to visitors, at times: Chinese and American—or, neither Chinese nor American—a matter of perspective.

Second Daughter

I was the second of four daughters. This birth position affected my life in major ways. My first autobiography, *Second Daughter*, deals in more detail with the painful effects of being the second of four daughters in a traditional Chinese home. In brief, traditional Chinese culture values boy children more than girls. There is a Chinese idiom that expresses this idea, which translates, literally, as 'heavy boys, light girls.' In an agrarian society where it was important to have boys to run the farm, it's clear why families—historically for thousands of years—have preferred boys. A boy would also carry on the family name; this is important in Chinese culture.

Another Chinese saying, "First the blossom, then the fruit" expresses the feelings of parents that if the first-born is not a boy, parents can still wait with nervous anticipation for the birth of their second child to have their dreams of a son realized. My mother saw herself as a failure for not having produced a male heir and in turn, she blamed me for the fact of my birth, mercilessly and constantly, for most of my life.

Much later, when I moved to America, I gave birth to my first child—a girl. The second was a boy. Both were adored and loved, as well as my third child, another daughter. However, I did not write to my mother in China to tell her that she had grandchildren, until my son was born. Such was my fear of her awesome wrath.

Modern science tells us that a child's gender is determined by the father's genes only. Imagine how much emotional pain and humiliation—heaped upon and borne by both mothers and daughters over centuries of tradition—could have been avoided had they been privy to this now common knowledge.

Hunan

In 1931, the Japanese bombed Manchuria, to the northeast of China. Invasion and occupation followed.

My childhood home was in the northeastern city of Peking. Manchuria was northeast, and the Pacific Ocean was immediately east, as was Japan. When I was six, the Japanese forces started to encroach upon Peking, and our family fled. We left on the last train to Tientsin (now Tienjin) before the

Japanese army marched into Peking (now Beijing). The family stayed only one day in Tientsin, a dingy industrial center, and then moved to a small town in the south. Within those twenty-four hours, the Japanese bombed the city three times.

Our next flight became a two-month journey, a thousand mile trek inland to Hunan province in southeastern China, where our ultimate destination was the home of my paternal grandfather. Father was warmly welcomed there as the son and family heir. The home of my grandfather was to be our refuge for a few long and ultimately uncomfortable years.

Grandfather was Buddhist; our family was Baptist. The strong personalities of my mother and grandfather almost guaranteed the resulting friction. In Grandfather's eyes, my parents were not really married, since they hadn't been married in a Buddhist ceremony. As the family patriarch, he made the rules and expected them to be obeyed without question. Soon after they arrived, he insisted that my parents get married in a Buddhist ceremony, a demand that, despite the fact that my sisters and I found this quite amusing, did not sit well with mother at all. Part of the marriage ceremony required a low bow, or *koutou*, to Grandfather. Although my willful mother acquiesced to this display of respect for her husband's father, this was only the beginning of her clash with Grandfather and his family.

I was dazzled by Grandfather's compound. The

main pavilion boasted a house with a bright red door and gleaming brass hardware, which opened to a courtyard shimmering with flowers and *koi* fish circling in the open pond. We stayed in one of the many impressive houses on the estate. I shared a lavishly appointed room with Alice, my older sister. I remember the walls glazed in pale green, with two richly carved and painted headboards for our twin beds, which were draped in bright red silk. Our beds were separated with a mahogany chest on which Alice kept her prized possession, a Chinese flute. I used it as a shelf for the many books that had been left for us. Although most of them were works of Chinese poetry, there were one or two books in English. One of them was *Gone with the Wind.* ("Kathie," my second husband Charles, used to tell me, "there's quite a bit of Scarlett O'Hara in you!")

I can't tell you why, but Grandfather took a special liking to me. He often took me out in his garden, a great pride in his life. The garden was truly magnificent and peaceful, a seemingly endless carpet of colors. He would point toward his prized magnolia trees anchoring both ends of the flower beds and say "Xiao-yen, can you see the white buds on those trees? And how beautiful are my pink and white peonies just starting to bloom?" We would stroll, noticing the windflowers, tulips, and endless seas of yellow daffodils. Now and then butterflies could be seen floating over the flowers, enjoying their sweet nectars.

I worshipped my grandfather. I loved being in

his presence. He was stately and witty, almost 70 years old. He wore a favorite blue robe with gold threads running throughout and projected an air of royalty, and I felt as if I was living with an old-world, scholarly mandarin. He spoke *with* me, and not to me. I listened, spellbound, as he instructed me in the sayings of the ancient sage Confucius. We discussed life lessons and the path of the righteous person. However strange it might have been that Grandfather had singled me out, I was thrilled that I could bask in his light and share his life. From him I received the attention and love denied me by my emotionally distant mother.

My need to please him was so strong that I made sure to read the books of Chinese poetry, in case a discussion arose. I even willingly—I think—drank the bitter Chinese medicine he prescribed for me when I became ill. I now attribute this newly found ability to please my grandfather as instrumental in relating to important and powerful people later in my life.

As was the style of the times, Grandfather had an opium den on his compound. He taught me, a nine year old, how to mix and prepare his opium pipe for him. I was both happy and proud that, of his four granddaughters, he chose me to assist him in his daily smoking ritual. My sisters and l constantly competed for Grandfather's love and affection. Lao Chang, the family cook who escaped Peking with us, and who I regarded as my best friend, always plotted with me to win this 'contest.' Our years in Hunan developed my desire to compete to win—losing was never my strong suit.

Grandfather had a number of concubines, girls young enough to be his daughter. From behind closed doors, muffled giggles and adult sounds came buzzing through the walls during his nightly rituals. It was never clear to me what was going on. I knew only that there was some strange connection between men and women. So it wasn't surprising that the concubines, too, would become a part of my life. I received instruction from the young girls in the seductive arts. They impressed upon me the importance of charming manners and subservience to men.

My mother, an educated person, turned a blind eye to these instructions and ministrations. She wanted to get ahead in life and in society, so she thought that being in Grandfather's good graces would advance her station. With her blessing, I was trained to clean the lutes that were used for nightly entertainment. I learned how to stir the inks that Grandfather used for his ornate calligraphy.

Many nights, I was awakened and had to report to my grandfather's chambers, merely to assist his concubines as they stirred the inks in preparation for his writings. I was there only as a mascot, an indication of his own control over his family. Later, when the concubines began to mix the sweet opium potion that he smoked well into the early hours of the morning, I would be dismissed. I'd return to my own bed, bleary-eyed and craving sleep, yet somehow proud that I had been singled out.

Looking back many years later, I understand how I was taken advantage of. My head was all mixed up! My values, so inappropriate! I never mentioned this episode in my life to my husband or to my own children, because I realized how awful and backward this all was. I think the main reason I have imposed strict prohibitions against drugs and alcohol to both my children and myself is because of Grandfather's opium addiction. To this day, I make friends who have just one drink at dinner feel uncomfortable.

In one of the rooms of his house, Grandfather had installed his own Buddhist temple. A long table was heaped with platters of fresh fruit and cooked Chinese food, and cushions were provided for those who wished to communicate with the gods. On religious holidays, Buddhist monks conducted the service. We always knew that something special was happening because the fragrant aroma of burning incense filled the compound.

Mother had a difficult time with Grandfather's religious beliefs and practices. Our family was Baptist and believed in the one true God. Buddhism, with its multiple deities, was anathema to her. Mother took her religion quite seriously and resented having to be in a house dominated by a religion that was so different from hers. During the Spring Festival, we had to pay our obeisance to Grandfather's personal Buddha statue. Mother refused to kneel.

In no time at all, mother had developed a

hatred of everything about the Hunan province. She hated the unintelligible Hunan dialect; she mocked it as a "jumble of murmured sounds." The simple, rural, southern Hunan culture and highly spicy cuisine were so different from what we were accustomed to in northern, cosmopolitan Peking. She regarded the Hunan people as ignorant, relics of the dark ages. But most importantly, she was a woman who was used to having her own way, and in Grandfather's house, she was having none of it. The fact that my mother could never be in charge led to a major conflict of personalities. We were guests seeking refuge in war-torn China, and mother was biting—sometimes viciously—the hand that was feeding us.

After a couple of long years, she'd had enough. "I am not staying here any longer," she announced. She urged father to look elsewhere, in faraway Chungking to our west, for a job and a place for us to stay. Mother wanted to leave Hunan as soon as possible and our ever-complaisant father agreed. The plan was for him to leave and to send for us later.

At that time, travel in rural China was fraught with danger. Warlords, pirates, kidnappers and bandits controlled the area, and father was not guaranteed a safe route. Several harrowing, nerve-frazzling months passed before we finally received a letter from him. The news wasn't good: the Yangtze River gorges were impassable in October, our planned time of parting. We would have to wait until spring.

I reflect on this time in Hunan, how our lives were being thrown into such emotional turmoil. I hated my father for leaving us. My mother was miserable without him. It was inconceivable that we had come from Peking, established on a modern Western campus where mother was admired and envied as the sophisticated wife of a well-respected professor. Hunan was the complete opposite, and the perceived backwards way of life exasperated my mother and frightened my sisters. They jumped at the slightest sound, and Alice hid in her bed most of the time nursing migraines. I was the only one who wholeheartedly embraced Hunan life. I did not, however, enjoy my relationship with my mother. I was so disappointed in her for not being able to cope with life at Grandfather's.

But Alice succinctly summed it up: "We just didn't belong."

Chungking

Spring of 1943 brought with it a more tamed Yangtze, so finally we set off to Chungking, the 'Mountain City,' 640 miles west of Hong Kong, known for its unbearably hot and humid summers and cold, foggy winters.

Mother was more than ready to leave. Despite the perils of a fatherless journey, she packed us up and we set off. For the first time in our lives, Mother was our leader. We were transported first by a litter carried by two servants, who took us to one of the Yangtze's shores. Grandfather's wealth and influence provided us with a thirty foot-long *sampan*, a flat-bottomed wooden boat with sails, waiting and ready to take us to Chungking. Our captain provided us with an able crew consisting of his sons and his wife as cook. We set sail three days later.

To a child's eyes, the river was a dark, bottomless mystery. Our nervousness was compounded by mother's shrill cautions: "Don't play around at the edge of the *sampan!* Don't fall over!" But before long, we were scampering about the deck like little buccaneers. I loved life on the boat. A sailor's life was hard work, but it was fascinating, and this new experience provided a welcome respite from the tension we had just left.

As we made our way up river, we enjoyed catching fish for our daily meals. The *sampan* was stocked with rice, vegetables, noodles, oil, and spices, including the eye-watering hot soy sauces that are the trademark of Hunan cuisine. Crew and passengers all ate together, family style, and mother even complimented the cook on the food she'd rejected just a few days ago. Maybe the spicy Hunan food tasted better on the water.

At dusk, the captain anchored the boat at a calm inlet, where the crew could rest after dinner and we would spend the night. The next morning, we would all jump into the water for a bath. Chang Ma, our family maid, used this time to wash our dirty clothing in the river. Once we had completed our morning ablutions, the captain ordered the sailors to pull up anchor and set sail again.

One early morning after a few days of voyage, I felt our boat come to a lurching halt. The crew quickly jumped into the water, tying heavy ropes around their waists, and started to pull the *sampan* to the shore. As they waded toward dry land, the captain explained to mother that the only way to get to shore was to haul our boat against the strong current. The shore rapidly drew nearer, and we spied a large group of people waiting for us with three carriages. "You are looking at Chungking," the captain announced.

We saw a man waving at us. "Could that be Father?" asked my younger sister, Victoria. "But his hair is so white!" exclaimed Alice. As we got closer, we recognized with shock that that man was, indeed, our father. In three months, his black hair had turned completely white, and he appeared to be so much older and thinner than when he had left us in Hunan. Mother gazed at him and gave him a light smile. No effusive kisses were thrown across the water. I suppose at that time social etiquette frowned on public displays of affection, but it was a magical moment for me when my parents' eyes locked. For the first time in my young life, I was witness to an overt expression of their love. Our family was reunited.

Father and Lao Chang gathered our belongings, and once again we had to take a ferry to get to the other side of the city of Chungking. When we complained, he said, "The Japanese have been bombing us 24 hours a day. It will be safer living on the south shore away from the city."

We were not prepared for the devastation of Chungking. Shacks were abandoned, bombed out roofs had gaping holes that resembled evil, toothless mouths. Charred buildings revealed no sign of life. We could barely breathe with open sewers and rotting corpses in the streets. As we neared the city we noticed houses painted black—"so they would not be noticeable to Japanese bombers," Father explained.

One more river crossing and a trek up a huge hill took us finally to our house, newly built by the government. As father presented our living quarters to the family, I could hear mother mutter under her breath, "I should have stayed in Hunan." For once, I agreed with her. Our new abode was no more than a mud shack with a straw roof perched on a huge mountain cliff. Our front 'yard' afforded us a vista of the Yangtze, hundreds of feet below. But unlike our mother, our disappointment was short-lived. We were safe, under our father's capable protection. It could have been worse!

Then reality set in. Summers were sweltering and winters bitter cold in the mountains. Like all the other refugees, we found life to be a constant struggle. We had no electricity or running water. Our water had to be lugged uphill from the city's main water supply. We had to use chamber pots, which had to be emptied regularly. Our beds lay on an earthen floor, each a wood plank covered with thin cotton padding. They were enclosed by netting to protect us from the bloodthirsty mosquitoes. If the mosquitoes didn't get you, the bedbugs would. And then of course we needed our daily quinine to prevent malaria.

Father secured for us a small plot of land, and I farmed with him, raising the vegetables that provided our meals. He never scolded me and treated me with the respect accorded a son; in fact, I felt it was my duty to make him proud the way a son would.

Life in Chungking took its toll on all of us. Frequent bombing raids by the Japanese forced us to scurry to the nearest caves for protection. But caves provided their own unexpected horrors. The severed limbs and bodies of my schoolmates killed during raids were stored and heaped one on top of one another on the dank cave floor. It became an almost daily occurrence: a friend one day would be lost to me forever the next.

One day we had big news! On our little transistor radio, we heard that the Japanese had bombed Pearl Harbor. On December 8, 1941, America entered the war. We wished it could have been sooner, but not one of us harbored any ill feelings about the United States' late entry into the war. In Chungking we listened with great sorrow and sympathy to President Franklin D. Roosevelt's "Day of Infamy" speech. Hope was in short supply, so we clung to his every word. Roosevelt made such a powerful impact on the Chinese people that when he died, a few years later, I joined my high school classmates in climbing to the top of a nearby mountain and lighting candles in his memory. Together we sang our tribute: "America the Beautiful."

High School

Life, in its newly diminished form, continued. My father's prior position as a professor at a university founded by Baptists opened to us the doors of the Faith Baptist Missionary School in Chungking. Alice and I were immediately enrolled; however, no sooner did we start our studies than mother withdrew me. She was displeased that the school downplayed the arts, so she enrolled me at Chungking's Academy of Performing Arts, where one of the instructors was a former student of Martha Graham. The school also had an academic program that heavily emphasized western culture, a fact not lost on my mother. Six months later, it became obvious that I was taking ballet and dance much more seriously that she had intended, so she pulled me out of that school and sent me back to the Baptist missionary school, claiming that it was dishonorable for a woman of our social status to perform in public.

Father also advised me to return to a more academic curriculum at the Baptist school. His thinking, unlike mother's, was consistent with the plan I had for myself: learn as much as possible and as quickly as possible, so that I might attend a nursing program at college and begin my chosen profession. So I didn't put up a fight with either of my parents, and I willingly returned to the Baptist high school.

My teachers at the missionary school thought

highly of my academic abilities, so they allowed me to skip a grade. I would be in the third year at school, the same as my older sister. I was thirteen years old at the time. My mother told me—in no uncertain terms—that she expected that I would do well and make her proud. In fact, I did well at school and cherished every minute there. Our academic curriculum included history, geography, art and calligraphy, for which we had Chinese instructors. English, health, mathematics, and science were taught by the missionaries. I also participated and excelled in many extracurricular activities. No one—not even my best friend there, Chang La-mei—knew what drove me to accomplish so much. I never admitted to her or to anyone that I needed to earn not only my mother's respect, but her affection as well. If only I worked hard enough, maybe she would love me.

A year later, Chang La-mei confided to me that one of her brothers had joined the communists. This was considered a treasonous act, and the news quickly became public. The next day, my best friend was expelled from school. I rebelled against her unfair treatment, speaking my mind to my classmates and to my history teacher. I objected that, in none of our history textbooks—not once—was the communist cause ever explained. The Chinese communists represented several million of our countrymen. What did they believe in? Why did they oppose our government? There were rumors that only the communist cadres offered effective resistance to the invading Japanese military, but this was not spoken of. It wasn't that I supported the communist position or party; I, like my classmates, was ignorant about national politics, but I needed to know more. Why wasn't anything explained to us? I also felt it unjust that Chang La-mei was being punished for an act committed by her brother, not herself.

In the end, though, it didn't matter what I had said. My friend was permanently expelled. I never saw her again.

My father must have had more influence than I'd thought. Despite my rebellious outbursts, I was permitted to remain and complete my school curriculum. I graduated in 1945, when I was fifteen.

Shanghai

Japan surrendered in 1945. Our exile in the mountains was over. We left Chungking without looking back and embarked on our final move within China, to Shanghai, "the Pearl of the Orient." We sailed on an American Liberty Navy ship from Chungking to Shanghai. The family, including our loyal remaining servants, carried all our worldly belongings up the gangway and onto the ship. On board, we each had a small, cramped space in which to sleep and a canteen with a bowl. For the entire trip, we ate and drank from those containers. I was introduced to U.S. Navy food. We didn't mind the cramped quarters and the lousy food, though; we were on our way to start a new, peaceful, hopefully better life. We would not miss the tasteless brown rice and sandy vegetables (To make more money, farmers would often add sand so the rice would weigh more). No more living like scavengers hunting for water and food with only bedbugs and lice as unwanted pets. No more sleeping in the same room with twenty other girls in school, dreading the sounds of bombings and air raids.

When we arrived in Shanghai, we were met by Uncle Lin, my mother's sister's husband, and my cousins who had lived and survived under Japanese occupation. Uncle Lin offered us the use of their old town house, which was located in one of the most prestigious parts of Shanghai. Mother, in her inimitable way, saw Shanghai as the city that would give her a dream life. "Xiao-yen," she trilled, "Life in Shanghai is living a millionaire's life without having a million." We were so excited to see the town house in which we would live. Father assigned us each a room. My youngest sister Joan and I shared a regular western-style bathroom. Lao Chang prepared a memorable celebratory dinner for us that night.

Father had a job waiting for him at Shanghai University. The city was recovering from years of Japanese occupation and Chinese air force bombing. As a result of the unequal treaties that China was forced to sign after the Opium Wars of mid-19th century, parts of Shanghai were controlled by western interests and governments. The Europeans had their own civil authorities and police, and Chinese were often prisoners in their own city. One day not long after we'd moved there, I came upon a nearby park. Eager to run around in wide-open spaces, I approached the park's entrance. A sign in English and Chinese barred me: "No Chinese or Dogs Allowed."

An Arranged Marriage

Disease and death had followed us from city to city during our escape and I now wanted to face them head on. I had to participate in the war's recovery efforts. I felt it was my duty to help the sick and needy. For a long time, I had wanted to attend college and go into the medical field as a doctor, but realized it would take much too long. I would be able help people more quickly as a nurse. In China, however, nursing was considered a low class occupation, and what's more, it was reserved for males only. My mother scoffed at my career choice: "Xiao-yen, it is shameful for a well-bred woman to touch the bodies of male strangers!" She insisted I go to medical school to become a doctor (a profession in which, for some reason, the shame of touching male bodies would magically disappear). I did not want to wait six or seven years to start my career: I wanted to help people *now*. The time for me to start giving back to society was way past due.

Mother, however, had other plans for my future. She was already arranging a marriage for me. Toward this end, it was important to her for me to know how to be presentable to the eligible bachelor who she would choose to be my mate. I had to learn to dress stylishly, cook, and master other homemaking skills, so I could attract, land, and keep a rich husband. I wanted none of it. Even as a teenager, I knew that these were not ingredients of happiness for a successful marriage.

Arranged marriages were common in China: the custom of dating didn't exist, and sometimes a marriage would be planned when the future bride and groom were just children. The marriage was considered more a business transaction between two families who hoped to benefit in some way. A typical arranged marriage could provide enhanced social status or some financial advantage. In my case, mother was looking out for herself. It was usually the son's responsibility in China to provide for the care, feeding, and security of his parents during their later years. Since I was the disappointing non-son, this responsibility fell on my shoulders. My mother was preparing me to take care of her in her old age.

There is no small bit of hypocrisy in the fact that my parents' marriage had not, in fact, been arranged. Father had been betrothed before he met my mother. According to Chinese custom, if a woman is brought across the threshold of a man's family home, the couple is considered automatically married. A young woman, a stranger to my father, had been brought over his family's threshold by his parents. The young couple was married in everyone's eyes—except for father's. Refusing the arranged marriage, he fled to the U.S. prior to the actual wedding ceremony. Father's actions brought intense shame to his family, and he was considered *persona non grata* for quite some time. The jilted woman, unable to deal with her shame, committed suicide a year later. Ultimately, father and mother met, fell in love, and got married, and his parents accepted the union.

This was so many years ago, and I am not sure if I knew the details of my parents' marriage before they arranged my own. I might have pushed back more firmly, I believe. As it was, however, it was a foregone conclusion that any opposition to mother's plans for my marriage would result in certain failure and my unhappiness. The tension between us was unhealthy for my family as well, so I settled for what I thought was a compromise between her and me. I told her that I would agree to the arranged marriage, as long as she would let me enter nursing school. I so enjoyed her outrage at my impudence. I dug my heels in and she finally agreed to the deal. She convinced herself that my career plan was a youthful indiscretion I would soon outgrow... how wrong she was!

Our compromise set, mother focused exclusively on me. She bought me high heels, stockings, jewelry, coats, and a complete selection of evening dresses. I was taught how to shake hands in a demure, feminine style, yet she counseled "Don't appear shy, otherwise, they'll think you're a backward country bumpkin." I was taught ballroom dancing—the fox trot, Peabody, Lindy hop, Viennese waltz, and my favorite, the tango. I felt that after suffering the indignities of Chungking, I was entitled to these luxuries.

Chang-Jui

The "Pearl of the Orient" was indeed a heavenly city. In 1947, I entered the Shanghai University School of Nursing, where I immersed myself in my studies. I did manage to take my nose out of the books to attend a few formal parties held by a colleague of father who had just returned to Shanghai from the U.S. He was head of a successful company and entertained Western businessmen who were looking to establish a foothold in Shanghai, as they recognized China's huge market potential. These lavish social events were hosted at Shanghai's Park Hotel. I wasn't surprised that my parents encouraged my attendance since the colleague had two eligible sons.

Mother and Father accompanied me to the first of these parties. Not long after we were seated, I met Chang-Jui, the handsome younger son. He came over to our table and asked for my mother's permission to dance with me. As he led me to the dance floor, he asked my name. "Catherine," I told him. He looked at me with intense eyes, "Catherine. A name easy to remember, but hard to forget." We danced for a while, and by the time we came back to our table, my mother had found out that Chang-Jui's brother had an impressive and influential position as Chiang Kai-shek's chief of staff. She also learned that Chang-Jui was on his way to the United States to study communication and political science at Columbia University.

"Oh, Xiao-yen," she whispered to me. "You have been dancing with one of the most desirable bachelors in all of China!"

The next morning, a courier delivered to me a box of delicate long-stemmed pink roses. While my experience at the dance was pleasant enough, and Chang-Jui's attentions flattering, I was still committed to my own ambitions. Mother was overflowing with excitement, and before long, she announced to me that I was formally engaged to Chang-Jui. I was sixteen and Chang-Jui, twenty-six. I was not allowed to reject the husband my parents had chosen for me and now I could no longer leave the house for any other social occasions. Dating someone else would be unthinkable. Mother's words resounded: "A well-brought-up Chinese lady may not socialize until she is married." In other words, I could no longer attend any student meetings or functions and I couldn't see friends without supervision. This edict affected me academically. If I wasn't allowed to take part in my nursing program's field trips to the countryside where I could receive real-life medical training, I wouldn't be able to graduate. My fate was sealed by mother's pronouncements and commands.

My last two years in Shanghai were filled with resentment and rebellion. I put up a big fight to protest the marriage. I threatened to run away, to kill myself, or even worse—to join the communist party! When I now think back on the temerity I exhibited as a teenager to reject the fate being imposed on me, I can't believe that I didn't suffer more severe consequences. Opposition to arranged marriages was unheard of, and death for the wayward daughter was a possibility. Fortunately, my parents didn't believe in the 'death option.' They were, however, a bit afraid of my threats and backed off somewhat. Mother agreed to let me go back to school. I was summoned to our living room and stood by the doorway, dreading the next thing that she would devise for home torture. "Xiao-yen, Father and I have decided to let you complete your studies, but you must promise not to attend any student meetings or participate in any street protests. As soon as you get your visa from the United States, you will go there and marry the man we have chosen for you."

For the first time ever, I was going to have to barter for my freedom. Bowing my head only slightly, I acceded. "Yes, Mother, I promise." Father came over to kiss and hug me and told me to take my sister Victoria out for a movie. I felt I'd been given a prisoner's release. Victoria and I joyfully went to see Katherine Hepburn in *Little Women*. Despite the conditions, I'd been granted *some* liberty.

The next day, my mother packed my suitcase and sent me to board at the nursing school. I loved being there. I received high grades, and before long, I was on the last and most exciting part of my training, field triage. All the students were sent to different rural areas around Shanghai. Since there was a severe shortage of doctors, we had to deliver babies, provide postpartum and neonatal care. We sutured lacerations, set broken bones, and treated snakebites, malaria, typhoid, and cholera.

During my triage training, I tried in vain to use father's influence to petition government officials for supplies. Later, the other nurses and I found out that our corrupt government officials were lining their pockets with American economic and humanitarian aid dollars while disease and starvation killed hundreds of residents every day. Before long, students were organizing protest marches against Chiang Kai-shek's government. Chiang's secret police were as brutal as any other dictator's, his henchmen beating and killing many protesters right on the street. I joined the marches whenever I could, sneaking away without my parents' knowledge. We demanded that Chiang Kai-shek step down and called for new presidential elections.

Meanwhile, there were more banquets. Chang-Jui and I talked. We danced. We got to know each other better. One night, during a Viennese waltz, he told me he loved me. He wanted me to accept the arranged marriage and join him in the U.S. He would be leaving for America in a few weeks, and if I hadn't agreed to be his wife by then, he said that he would write me daily.

Chang-Jui returned to the U.S. and true to his word, for an entire year, I received love letters daily, sometimes twice in one day. One day I received a package, a two-carat diamond engagement ring. The enclosed letter read, "I'm asking you to marry me. Please consider it. And even if you don't love me now, Catherine, I think I can make you love me eventually."

Civil War

China was being torn apart by civil war—the communists were waging war against the Nationalist government. The United States aided the Nationalists, led by Chiang Kai-shek, with massive economic support, but the Nationalist bureaucracy was rife with political corruption. The Chinese people suffered so intensely throughout the country that they turned against the Nationalist party.

In 1948 the news of the advance of the communist party sent widespread fear throughout Shanghai. There were runs on the banks; people tried, in vain, to convert their Chinese paper currency into gold. Inflation was uncontrollable. I remember carrying suitcases of almost worthless Chinese money just to buy groceries. Much of the Shanghai populace was fleeing *en masse* hoping that the communist army could be eliminated from the major eastern cities. Their hopes were in vain: "The People's Revolution" couldn't be ignored any longer.

The communist forces had taken Peking and Tientsin; Nanking, the southern capital of China, was sure to be next. Defeat was inevitable. I didn't support the communists, but at the same time, I hated the corruption and brutality of the Chiang Kai-shek government. Chiang's army was not popular with the people, especially those in the countryside. Under martial law declared by Chiang, the army was free to loot, rape young girls and women, and savagely beat or kill local citizens without reason.

37

Yet we were young and naïve. We still thought that democracy and freedom would win out at the end of the war.

As a young college student, I'd joined the student movement protesting Chiang's corruption and his imposition of martial law. I would sneak out through my bedroom window without a second thought. We'd gather in large groups and discuss China's political dilemmas until the early morning hours, when I'd sneak back home, exhausted yet energized. My parents never knew I left the house.

One day in 1945, government soldiers came and arrested father. They charged him as a communist sympathizer, accusing him of consorting with the "enemies of the Republic." This was not the United States. In China, a man was considered guilty until proven innocent. I asked family members and some of father's university colleagues for assistance to protest the charges. We appealed, and the authorities dropped the charges. Father returned home, but this incident had far-reaching effects. When the exodus began a few years later to escape the communist takeover, father and mother were not able to obtain visas. Their fates had been sealed.

The day after I graduated from nursing school, father took me into his study. With great sadness, he informed me that it was time for me to leave Shanghai for the United States. "Everything is arranged," he whispered. The betrayal left me speechless. Not only was I devastated that things had been planned for me without my knowledge, but I was also very patriotic. I found my words quickly.

"I won't leave my country!"

Father's eyes were moist. "You need to learn more about your chosen career—and experience life—so you can come back to help China rebuild. Mother has packed an elegant trousseau for you in case you decide to marry Chang-Jui. We are also giving you one of our family heirlooms, a tapestry passed down from your grandfather. One day you might need to sell it to raise money to support yourself." I wondered about that statement: was he not confident that I would go through with the marriage? Maybe he knew me better than I'd thought.

He continued, "Our side is losing. The communist army has already taken Peking. It will be a matter of weeks or even days before they enter Shanghai, and that will end our way of life forever. I have been working hard for you to obtain your exit permit."

I didn't want to accept the fact that my father's description of Shanghai's imminent fate was correct. Naïvely, I offered my own perspective. "Father, I cannot leave Shanghai right now. I don't think the Red Army can reach us here. After all, Shanghai is China's most populous and dynamic city. We have our own strong army to defend us. And besides, haven't you always told me that we could overcome all adversity as long as our family sticks together?"

He took my hand. "Remember Catherine, China did not really win the war. It was the Allies who freed us from the Japanese. Our government's army is weak—no tanks, and no airplanes. Chinese people are naturally not supportive of Chiang Kai-shek's corrupt government. Don't you remember the Rape of Nanking? Our army was helpless to stop it!"

How could anyone forget that day? December 13, 1937—thousands of Chinese were raped and murdered in a single day. At the time, father was working as a historian-scholar in Chungking. He heard firsthand reports from many of the survivors who had escaped the carnage and mass murder of innocent civilians. According to the accounts my father heard, the Japanese Royal Army had marched into Nanking. They went door-to-door and randomly raped and killed hundreds of innocent Chinese people without provocation. They destroyed important Chinese art, as well as historical sites. In six weeks of unfathomable terror, the Japanese eradicated a thousand years of Chinese history.

What my father couldn't tell his teenage daughter I discovered for myself years later. There were eyewitness accounts of women who were brutally raped, their bodies mutilated with swords or penetrated with bayonets or bamboo sticks before their murders. Young children were targets as well, their bodies split open while they were still breathing.

Our family probably escaped a horrific fate by packing and moving constantly from one town to the next. My father's decision not to live in any Japanese occupied town kept us alive; however, our constant fear and vigilance took a physical and emotional toll on us all.

Those hasty escapes still haunt me on sleepless nights.

During those years, father had been our family hero—my hero—our leader, carefully planning and leading us away from dangerous places. It had seemed as if we were constantly holding our breath until we were out of danger. Relief had been short-lived. I understood what my father was trying to tell me. One stayed in China at one's peril.

Father believed this environment was dangerous for a free spirited and outspoken young Chinese woman like me. Mother's plan was for me to marry Chang-Jui Shen, the answer to all her prayers. Their motives might have been different but their goals were the same. I was to go to the United States.

Since my father's previous arrest denied my parents visas, I was the only one in the family who might have a chance to get a visa to go to the United States. The man I was supposed to marry lived in New York and was trusted by the Chinese government. Father read that there was a nursing shortage in the U.S., and he was certain that my medical skills would ensure my successful immigration. They all hoped that I would do well there and later send for the whole family. I would never know whether I could love Chang-Jui unless we were with each other for some time, on our own terms, and were together in another place. There seemed to be no alternative: I was to go to America.

There were long lines at the American Consulate passport bureau, where people waited endlessly to obtain a visa. Fortunately, the red tape was cut for us.

"I left China as an 18-year-old and arrived in the U.S. as a 23-year-old!"

Father had a connection with Dr. Leighton Stuart, former president of Yenching University and currently the U.S. ambassador to China. My travel documents and airline tickets were expedited. He issued me a working visa, so that I would be able to work and support myself in America. We were extremely fortunate to have friends in high places.

But now we faced another obstacle: my future husband's brother opposed our marriage. He felt that his brother could do better than me, merely a low-class nurse, for a wife. He tried to stop me from getting a passport, using a little-known technicality that prohibited minors under the age of twenty-one from leaving the country unless accompanied by an adult. Thank goodness for Father's connections! He spoke to another friend, an official even higher up in the Chinese government than the brother and within two days my birth certificate was altered. On April 17, I was eighteen years old. Two days later, I was twenty-three. "You will never forget your *real* age, Catherine," my father said to me, as he handed me my forged papers, "just remember you were born in the Year of the Horse."

By 1949, it was clear that the communists, under the leadership of Mao Zedong, would soon be the victors in China's civil war. Chiang Kai-shek, president of the Republic of China moved thousands of his Nationalist troops and two million refugees to Taiwan where he formed a government in exile, and vowed to continue the fight against the communists from the island province. Their rallying call was "Return to the mainland!" The communist forces were ultimately victorious however, and on October 1949, the People's Republic of China was formally established with its capital at Beijing, formerly Peking. Their goal was to retake Taiwan. No one imagined that after the communists took over China, diplomatic relations and direct communication between China and the U.S. would be cut. It would be almost 32 years before I would be able to see my family again.

A World of Change

Leaving China

*"Wheresoever you go,
go with all your heart."*

—Confucius

My heart was filled with enormous guilt as I left my loved ones and walked up the passageway onto the airplane. Goodbyes were impossibly sad. Their tear-stained faces would be seared in my memory for decades.

I boarded the Northwest Airline plane bound for New York City via Anchorage, Alaska. I was one of the lucky ones. Other Chinese citizens tried to escape via ship, but at least one ship of which I am aware capsized and many lives were lost. The trip from Shanghai to New York took more than twenty-eight hours, an eternity in the air. I kept telling myself to be brave and that things would be fine when I reached New York City. After all, I spoke fluent English. I'd read *Gone with the Wind!* But when the flight attendants announced our descent and arrival in New York I looked out my window and the city took my breath away. Imposing skyscrapers to my right, the bridges and the East River to my left—and so many lights! It hit me full force then: I was starting my new life, in a new country, a new world, with (probably) a new husband.

Chang-Jui met me at the airport. I had never

been so happy to see a familiar face. He said he would get a room for me at Columbia University's International House where he was a student, unless I decided to marry him right away. But I wanted to meet and adjust to America on my own terms. Although I already had my Chinese nursing degree, it wasn't recognized in the U.S. So the following week I enrolled in an undergraduate program at Mount Sinai Hospital in New York. Since I had minored in political science in college, Columbia University gave me a job in their political science research department. No more barriers to my new life—or so I thought.

When Mao Zedong formally announced the formation of communist China in October, 1949, the U.S. and The People's Republic of China broke all diplomatic relations. Their ensuing cold war suddenly left stranded all the Chinese people who came to the U.S. as students. They were people without a country. Chang-Jui had a scholarship at Columbia in communications and political science, but the communist takeover in China effectively cancelled it, so he needed to get a job. With only a student visa, his only job option was to work for the Taiwan nationalist Chinese government. He found employment in Washington DC, working as the administrative assistant for the Chiang Kai-shek government's military attaché. He began work there while I remained in New York.

I Do?

We were married in a Baptist church in New York once Chang Jui returned from Washington. As soon as the minister pronounced us husband and wife, I reflected on the fact that I had married without love or passion.

My reasons were simple and straightforward. This was the era of Joseph McCarthy and the "Red Scare." As a newly arrived immigrant, I was a suspect, simply because I had relatives who lived on mainland China. Chinese Americans were afraid to communicate with their families and loved ones abroad. My telephone was tapped; my mail was censored. The F.B.I. was routinely interrogating me. Despite my innocence, I was constantly afraid of being deported back to communist China, where the harsh new regime was causing untold pain and suffering among its people. Literally millions were persecuted; torture, hard labor, famine and execution were daily occurrences. Mao's regime was particularly hard on the older generation. I was not aware until I returned to China 30 years later that my father had been forced into working as a street cleaner. One of my sisters was sent to the countryside to work in a labor camp and my adored sister Alice lost an eye. I was powerless to help them during this time.

So it seemed like marriage could provide a safe haven for me. I didn't have to worry about the possibility of being sent to an internment camp like many

Japanese-Americans during WW II. Along with the security of marriage, I also had the good fortune to be assisted by my husband's brother (yes, that same one who didn't approve of our marriage) who was working in the diplomatic corps in the U.S. for the Chiang Kai-shek government in Taiwan. He convinced the U.S. State Department that I represented no threat to the country's security, and I was removed from the blacklist.

I know that these were not virtuous reasons for marrying someone, but nevertheless I heard myself utter "I do" in the presence of the minister, Chang-Jui, and our friends. I finally felt safe from Senator McCarthy, but I was now committed to a loveless marriage.

I received a new passport with my new name, Katherine Shen, born in 1925. At times, I was ashamed that I married Chang-Jui for less than noble reasons. But I had been honest with him about my feelings from the beginning. His response was, "Katherine, in time you will learn to love me." Like a gentleman, he told me that if I did not learn to love him after ten years, he would grant me a friendly divorce. Unlike other arranged marriages, I had met Chang-Jui before I married him, and I admired, respected, and even liked him. He was a scholar in both English and Chinese literature; he had studied the theologies of Confucianism, Buddhism, Judaism, and Christianity, and had attained great understanding. He had majored in political science and received a master's degree in journalism. He was a good man. Arranged marriages had worked for thousands of years in many countries, I reasoned—maybe it would work for me, too.

As young marrieds, we lived in an apartment that was located on beautiful Connecticut Ave in Washington, where most of the diplomats and their staff lived. I loved living in DC with its rich history and wealth of historical monuments. I especially loved the Lincoln monument because I admired the values that Abraham Lincoln stood for. It was important to find some stability in my life. I had suffered through the Japanese invasion and Chinese civil war. Now I faced new challenges: I was pregnant and without any means of contributing to our growing family. Chang-Jui and I had a hard time making ends meet, even with free rent at the diplomats' residence. Chang-Jui needed to find a new, better paying job.

One day, I read in *The New York Times* that the United Nations was looking for translators and interpreters. I showed the article to my husband and told him that I had already mailed an application for him to take the qualifying exam. Initially, he objected, and made excuses for not taking the exam. I knew that even though he was brilliant and passing would not be a problem, he was afraid of failing and felt that if he didn't do well, it would be a tremendous loss of face for him. His fears were unrealized: Chang-Jui passed with flying colors. He quit his job in Washington and we moved to New York, where he began his new job as a translator for the United Nations.

Ada

My first pregnancy was difficult. Despite wrenching morning sickness, I gained forty pounds. I was sticky and miserable all the time. I missed my old body. But I also looked forward to meeting my baby and being a mother.

Chang-Jui presented, in no uncertain terms, his demands for naming our child. He said that if the baby were a girl, he would name her. This would be my 'punishment' for not giving him a boy. If the child were a boy, then I could name him—my 'reward.' People asked me why I didn't stand up to my husband's rules. I only fought battles I knew I would win. This was a traditional Chinese marriage where the wife was subordinated to the whims and dictates of the husband. Fighting with Chang-Jui would have been useless. He wanted me to remain as I was when I was a naïve eighteen year old. He reminded me that good Chinese wives should stay home, cook, clean, and take care of their children

Our first child was born in Garfield Hospital in DC. When I awoke after the delivery, the nurse told me that my child was a beautiful girl with jet-black hair, weighing eight pounds and three ounces. "Your husband is waiting outside to see you," the nurse continued. Chang-Jui entered the room, and gently kissed me on the forehead. I returned his kiss, smiling weakly. "Sorry, Chang-Jui. I did not give you a son." His response was as expected. "I have named our girl Ada."

While Chang-Jui was trying to find a way to notify my parents in China, I was in no hurry. I anticipated my mother's response to the birth of a granddaughter. I was in no condition to accept her blame and censure.

Three days after Ada's birth, Chang-Jui brought us both home from the hospital. My husband carried Ada in the *blue* blanket up the two flights of stairs to our tiny attic apartment. I followed them. Suddenly, I became nauseated and weak-kneed. The ceiling spun and I hit the floor. I woke up, sometime later, in my own bed, and I started to doubt myself. Fainting was not a good sign for a homecoming. Was I going to be capable of being a fit mother to my daughter?

But I was proud to discover that mothering came easy to me. Ada usually cried after being put in her crib at night. I found that I was able to soothe her just by picking her up and gently rocking her back and forth. Looking at my beautiful daughter's smile, I knew that she was not *just* a girl.

We returned to New York eagerly. I promised myself I was going make the most of this famous cosmopolitan city. I wanted the perfect family, a rewarding career, and some adventure in my life. With Chang-Jui's new job, we could now afford our own place. A United Nations liaison officer advised us to move to Parkway Village, a rental garden apartment complex in Queens, N.Y. It was built for the United Nations staff and their families, many of whom had faced racial discrimination when they looked for housing in other areas. I loved living there from the start. It was a melting pot of different nationalities and cultures. On any given day I could hear languages from all over the world as Ada and I took our daily strolls in the park. Here, then, my daughter could experience a similar multicultural atmosphere to the one in which I'd spent my childhood.

Chang-Jui, however, was still uncomfortable living in a foreign country. But where could we go? Returning to mainland China was not possible, and while Taiwan would provide us with safety, it was not really home. Chang-Jui was lucky that he had not lived in China during the civil war; however, years of strife had made him lose hope for a bright future. He was not sure that he wanted to stay in the United States and make a go of it here. "Katherine, we should really go back home to serve our own country," he said. I knew my husband wanted to maintain our cultural values and traditions, and pass them onto our children. He never really tried to fit into American society but instead preferred to eat Chinese food and read Chinese books. He often felt confused about who he was and where he belonged. With the birth of Ada, and later, her siblings, we both had to agree on the way we wanted our children to see themselves. As soon as they were old enough, I would sit them down and tell them "When you look in the mirror, you will see a face that is 100% Chinese, but realize that you are also 100% American. Remember the richness of your Chinese heritage but always be proud to be an

American—never take life in this free country for granted."

Our major disagreement on the subject of child rearing, however, was religion. Chang-Jui did not believe in God the way I did. He thought that God resides in the heart, so there was no need for us to go to church or for the kids to go to Sunday school. He refused to have our children receive any religious training. My feelings about God were simple: "I see beautiful flowers. *Someone* must be in charge."

I wanted our children to learn about God and to make their own religious choices. They were American citizens; they should have the freedoms entitled to them by birth. Chang-Jui wanted them to know about their Chinese roots. After countless arguments, we compromised: the children would go to a Chinese school on Sunday instead of formal religious school. There, they could learn, not only the Chinese language, but also the Chinese way of life. I rationalized this accord by telling myself that in this way the children would have the full benefit of being bi-cultural.

Bringing up Ada was a complete joy. I was so young when I had her that I felt we were growing up together. She was a baby boomer, growing up in prosperous times. As soon as she could think for herself, Ada wanted to work and help the poor and less fortunate. At thirteen, she organized and raised money for the blind. She had a beautiful voice, and loved music and singing. For her 16th birthday, I bought her a guitar and hired a guitar teacher for her. Those were the Beatles days and she would often play and sing my favorite song, "Yesterday."

Ada always excelled in school. She was admitted to Tufts University in Boston, where she was even crowned homecoming queen! Chang-Jui and I hoped she would meet a nice Chinese boy in college and fall in love. Instead, she fell in love with a nice Jewish boy named Kenneth.

This is how Ada remembers it.

> "My parents wanted me to go to college in Boston because they heard from the Chinese community 'grapevine' that there would be a lot of smart, eligible Chinese boys there. While that turned out to be true, the problem was that these guys would ask me to marry them on the first or second date, so that was not going to happen! (Laughter)."[1]

We thought her infatuation was puppy love, and only realized how serious it was when we received an unexpected telephone call from Kenneth's parents. They were upset about Ada and Kenneth's relationship, and were looking for allies to help break them up. I told them that Ada and Kenneth had my support, as long as they finished college.

I didn't realize at the time how serious it was when a Jewish child married outside of the faith until my relationship many years later with my third husband, Henry, who was Jewish. Only then could I understand and appreciate how hard it must have been for Kenneth's parents to accept their relationship. Their courtship was turbulent—an American Chinese girl dating a Jewish boy was simply not accepted in society at that time. This was around the time the movie *Guess Who's Coming to Dinner* was released. The movie plot underscores prejudice and interracial marriage; I think the words were "they had a pigmentation problem." Ken's parents were so distraught that they sat *shiva* for their son who had ceased to exist, in their view, because he was dating a non-Jewish woman.

After seven years of dating, Ada and Kenneth were married by a rabbi at the United Nations Chapel in New York. Their wedding was simple but beautiful, with seventy-five guests, including Kenneth's parents.

After graduation, Ken attended medical school and received a residency position in Seattle, specializing in pediatric rehabilitation. He went on to become one of the most respected pediatric rehabilitation professors to teach and practice at the Children's Hospital in Seattle.

Ada attended law school and secured a position as a legal service attorney, working for social justice in Seattle, as well. They loved Seattle for its beautiful landscape and its multi-cultural diversity. They were a handsome couple—young, idealistic, energetic, and eager to save the world, and they have lived their lives accordingly.

Ada and Ken celebrated their 50th wedding anniversary in 2022.

The Nurse

Chang-Jui commuted to Manhattan from our residence in Queens each day. I stayed home and tried to be the perfect housewife. I re-created the favorite family dishes that Lao Chang had prepared. Money was still tight. I purchased inexpensive furniture at thrift stores, which I reupholstered myself. But soon I became restless. I wanted to conform to the role my husband had defined for me but I felt so isolated! Life had more in store for me, I was certain. I needed a career. Chang-Jui was dead-set upon hearing this. He insisted on total control. "We are doing fine as a family," he told me. "I want my wife to stay home, take care of my children, and attend to me when I come home. You do not need a career." I insisted, "But what about *my* hopes and dreams?"

After months of my nagging and wheedling, Chang-Jui eventually relented and allowed me to go into nursing, as long as my job did not interfere with my duty as a wife and mother. I promised to work the graveyard shift, so that I could be home during the day to perform my wifely duties.

One must understand that for Chang-Jui, it was a huge loss of face—both in his eyes and to other old-world Chinese—to have his wife work. It signified that he was unable to support his family. Other members of New York's Chinese community of the 1950s and 60s also exerted a lot of pressure on me to honor tradition and subsume my own career to that of my husband. My working would reflect poorly upon my husband, a United Nations translator. My major role as his wife was to enhance his career potential.

For me, though, it wasn't a question of income. We weren't impoverished. As a nurse, I just wanted to help people in need. It was my way of giving something back. First I'd grown up in a world of privilege, and then I saw the world as it really was. But I'm not going to deny that working added meaning to my life. I took, and passed, the nursing boards, which allowed me to work as a nurse in New York. Chang-Jui and I coexisted as husband and wife, and we shared three wonderful children. Each day we went our separate ways, enjoyed our own careers and individual lives, with our three children as our bond.

My first nursing job in New York was at the Hillside Mental Hospital in Queens. I took the graveyard shift so I could be home during the day to take care of our children, and cook and clean for the family. My next-door neighbor worked in that hospital as a supervisor and she gave me a lift each night to work.

My initial joy was quickly replaced with the awful realization that the hospital patients lacked adequate psychiatric or hygienic care. Typical treatment would be large doses of sleeping pills to maintain quiet. The whole hospital reeked of urine. By the end of my first week, I knew that this was not what I wanted in nursing. I resigned and became a special duty nurse at two hospitals simultaneously—the North Shore Hospital and Long Island Jewish Hospital, both on Long Island. I reported to whichever hospital required my services at any particular time—as long as it was during the graveyard shift.

After a few months, this grueling routine was getting to me. I was constantly exhausted. Once I almost fell asleep while driving home. I started having nightmares. Memories of the war haunted me like never before. I'd wake up sweating, gasping for air, terrified I might never see my family in China again.

The nightmares ended abruptly as soon as I started working in the emergency room. I'd approached my administrator, requesting the change, for I wanted to work in an atmosphere that needed quick response and action. Triage occupied my mind completely.

My work as an ER nurse came to the attention of two visiting medical doctors from Idlewild (now JFK) International Airport, Dr. Leon Starr and his partner, Dr. Louis Abelson, whose triage work for airplane disasters had brought them national recognition. They needed a nurse with my skills and competence, and I was hired. The Idlewild facility was a small triage medical center, housed in a Quonset hut. I loved my job; I thrived on the high pressure, life-and-death situations. I worked tirelessly, coming up with new ideas to make the practice more efficient. I went from staff nurse to assistant director of nurses and then to director of nurses.

Kathie, second from the left, and her nursing colleagues, review plans for the new hospital at John F. Kennedy International Airport.

After Idlewild became JFK Airport, I became administrator of the new, larger hospital built to accommodate it. Our patients included crash victims, firefighters, policemen, pilots, flight attendants, passengers, maintenance ground crews, and their families. We delivered babies, repaired bone fractures, and performed surgery in our operating room that did not require general anesthesia. But we weren't always tending to crash victims. One day, there were screaming, screeching sounds coming from the airport grounds. It was the Beatles! We had to set up emergency riot procedures to treat the teenage fans who'd been trampled while hoping to catch a glimpse of their idols. JFK is an international airport, and my proximity to it gave me the opportunity to meet celebrities like Jackie Kennedy and Judy Garland, among others.

Our emergency clinic became so popular we were treating hundreds of patients each day, yet I was still a mother with young children, wife, seamstress, cook, and cleaning lady. One winter evening, while eating dinner with my family, I received an emergency call: "Kathie, we had a major plane crash on the roadway near Far Rockaway Blvd. Several passenger cars were hit. There are survivors. How quickly can you get out here?" I was in my uniform in two minutes. It was snowing heavily, and the police escorted me to the crash site.

Oily, metallic fires burned all around the plane. I joined the doctors in their grim efforts. Fire fighters yelled to us to rescue victims who were bleeding, in cardiac arrest. One young woman was burned beyond recognition, screaming in pain: her car had been hit during the emergency crash landing. We performed emergency protocols before she was rushed to a nearby hospital.

Because of the bad weather, it took a lot longer for the ambulances and other emergency vehicles to arrive. The fires and wails of pain were hellish. It took hours before all the victims were transported to nearby hospitals.

We couldn't save everyone. A temporary morgue was established. The hardest part for me was bearing witness to life's excruciatingly painful realities. No matter how hard you try, no matter how fine your intentions, human loss is inevitable.

Ada remembers, "She was a standout as a nurse... I can still recall front page newspaper photos of my mother in her nurse's uniform, performing medical triage at airplane crash sites." [2]

Larry

I gave birth to our second child less than a year after our move to New York. He was born at St. John's Hospital. Before I went into labor, I had prayed that my next baby would be a boy. How ignorant and sad to think that giving birth to a son would solve all my life's problems.

I was filled with unimaginable pride—and gratitude—that I had finally produced a son for my husband. Although I rarely cried, tears streamed down my face as I named him Lawrence, after a character from my favorite *Little Women*. He never liked that name, so he became Larry. Back in China, my mother's friends had taunted her, "Your family doesn't know how to produce a son." I would not inform my mother of Ada's birth until Larry was born. Then, expecting redemption, we sent my parents a letter with news of both births.

Larry had severe childhood asthma. At night he woke up fighting for breath, and I suffered with him. Chang-Jui blamed me for Larry's condition, saying the disease was inherited from my side of the family. I had given him, in his estimation, a not-so-perfect son.

Unlike his sister, Larry had to struggle to maintain a "B" average in school. In our family, "A" was the only acceptable grade. I dreaded receiving Larry's report cards and Larry dreaded showing them to his father. He'd present them and warn, "Dad, I know you want me to have As on my report card, but we are in America. "B" is not that bad." Chang-Jui, however, would not accept any excuses.

When Larry became a teenager, he grew his hair long as an act of rebellion—I would chase him around the house with a pair of nurse's scissors, trying to cut it. When I wasn't chasing him, however, we enjoyed each other's company immensely—we both loved to cook. We spent hours cooking together. Many of Larry's friends became our official taste-testers, and Larry became one of the most popular boys in our neighborhood. Besides cooking, we went skating, and sometimes to Yankee Stadium, where the New York Yankees ruled the baseball world.

Despite the nightly asthma attacks that left him drowsy each morning, Larry studied hard and was admitted to Wittenberg University in Ohio. When it was time for him to go off to college, I regarded my tall, handsome son with pride. I felt confident he would achieve success, and this made it easier to let him go.

Larry graduated with a major in criminology, and in less than a week he found a job as a probation officer in Dayton, Ohio. Two masters' degrees in criminology followed, as well as a brief, childless marriage that ended in an amicable divorce.

Two years later, Larry fell in love with Debbie, a co-worker in his office. She was lovely and caring, and soon the couple married and bought a house in Ohio, where they still live.

Debbie and Larry are recognized by all who know them as kindred spirits; they have a genuine rapport. I was so happy that Larry finally found true love and happiness. The couple worked successfully in criminology until they retired. When people would ask me what their business was, I would jokingly reply, "They are in the crime business—and unfortunately, business is going up every year!"

Despite all the disagreements Larry had growing up with his father, he respected and cared for him deeply. When Chang-Jui suffered a severe spinal injury later in his life, years after our divorce, Larry attended to his father with devotion.

New York

Living in New York and raising two youngsters was a challenge. Money was tight, and I used all my resources to make sure they were well educated and cultured. Whenever I'd saved a few dollars, we would get tickets to inexpensive Broadway shows and concerts at the New York Symphony Hall. We took advantage of anything that was free! We were fortunate to attend performances by legendary artists like Arthur Rubinstein and Isaac Stern. When the pianist Van Cliburn came to New York to perform at the United Nations, Chang-Jui was able to get two tickets. Ada and I still talk about that incredible performance.

My neighbor Ruth Shoulders introduced me to the 42nd Street Public Library— the greatest library in New York. The first time I took Ada and Larry, their mouths formed perfect little "o's" at the sight of the two imposing stone lions guarding the tall brass doors! Once we entered, the cavernous halls, filled floor to ceiling with mountains of books—all for our use—was overwhelming.

The public library gave us the ability to visit the whole world for free. I introduced my children to China, promising them a 'real' visit someday. I had the pleasure of reacquainting myself with Louisa May Alcott and *Little Women*, and discovering other great female authors—Charlotte Brontë and Jane Austin among them.

My children also had a unique advantage: they had the opportunity to visit their parents' unusual workplaces. They loved coming to the bustling airport on school holidays. Ada remembers:

> "...We could go to the airport medical office and spend the day dispensing aspirin into tiny envelopes and playing with medical equipment ... In those days, the airport was an exciting and glamorous place where everyone knew and loved my mother—she was a celebrity!"[3]

Many kids in New York take field trips to the United Nations building, but for Ada and Larry, it was just "where our father works." Ada continues,

"... When the United Nations was in recess, we had our run of the place. We played tag in aisles of the UN General Assembly, put on multilingual headphones and pretended we were simultaneous interpreters. We watched nightmare-inducing films about how the World Health Organization, UNESCO and UNICEF were working to lessen the ravages of poverty, and then we would slide down the long banisters of the Secretariat. Best of all, we would be taken to the United Nations cafeteria, where we got our first taste of buttery croissants made by a French master baker!" [4]

Ava

When Larry was three, I became pregnant with our third child. By the third trimester, the exhaustion of work and my responsibilities as a mom took its toll. On one of my trips to the laundry room, I fell down a flight of stairs, hurting my back and hip. Because of my pregnancy, I couldn't take any pain medication. There was no one to replace me, either as a mother or a nurse, so I carried on.

One morning in September 1954, I woke up early and knew it was time to go to the hospital. When Chang-Jui brought me to the emergency room, I was fully dilated. The only problem was that Ava's head was in the wrong position for a natural birth. In the delivery room my doctor patted my hand. "Look Kathie, I am going try to turn the baby's head towards the birth canal. If that doesn't work, we will have to do a Caesarean section." I tried to look brave. "Please try. I want a natural childbirth for this baby." It took the doctor and me six hours of hard work before Ava was in the right position for a natural birth. I remember screaming until I passed out. When I awoke, I heard Ava's first cry... music to my ears.

Chang-Jui, Kathie, Ada and Ava

Bringing up Ava was a totally different experience. She was a sensitive, shy little girl but Ada describes her differently now that they are adults. "Ava is tougher than she looks. She is a very strong person who has a great perspective on life."

65

Both she and Ada were exquisite girls. Ava loved to read, listen to music, and watch television with me. Our favorites were ice skating programs and old movies. I was a mature mother by the time she was in her teens. All of her friends were envious of her looks and her academic abilities, and she became a fashion trendsetter in high school. She studied Chinese, dance and piano lessons, but did not pursue them later as an adult. She was an "A" student and tested especially strong in the sciences. But her interests lay elsewhere.

By the time Ava entered high school, both of her siblings were away at college. It was becoming obvious to Ava that her father and I were having marital problems. We thought that having another child would bring us closer together, but to no one's surprise, it didn't. Chang-Jui was often away from home, and I worked more than I had to. Finally, he and I agreed to divorce. Our verbal pre-nuptial agreement had made allowance for a no-fault divorce if our arranged marriage didn't work out, and I appreciate the fact that Chang-Jui respected this.

I did not have had the courage until many years later to tell the children that I was never in love with their father, that our marriage, in fact, had been arranged by our parents. We had hoped that in time, love would develop. While a divorce in a loveless marriage seemed logical to me, especially when I wanted a life for myself, it made our children, especially Ava, miserable. She adored her father! I'm certain I broke her heart by leaving him.

For months, she barely spoke to me. Even to this day, I feel guilty that I put my own happiness ahead of Ava's. Ada and Larry, too, were not happy with the idea of their parents splitting up. I had hoped that their being older and living on their own would make the adjustment easier. It probably did not.

Yet despite her tumultuous home situation, Ava graduated as valedictorian of her high school class. Like her older sister, she enrolled at Tufts University, but after two years she dropped out to find herself. She traveled to Taipei, Taiwan to stay with her uncle, the Foreign Minister for Chiang Kai-shek's government, to study Chinese, but she stayed there for only six months. She received a scholarship to study horticulture in Hawaii, and she was off again.

When Ava returned, she gave me the chance to be her mother again. We jogged each morning near the East River, went to many concerts and Broadway shows, watched old movies, danced to music, and enjoyed each other's company, just as we did when she was young. I felt some redemption for putting her through the trauma of the breakup. I thought ours was a relatively good divorce, but there is no such thing as a good divorce when you have children.

By this time I had married Charles Wei, and Ava was staying with us in our New York apartment. One day, she informed us that she had enrolled at the University of California at Davis, all the way across the country! I supposed that living in the same city with two divorced parents might have been too much for her to handle; she loved her father, so perhaps having a good time with her mother and stepfather made her feel just a little guilty.

Ava graduated with honors, majoring in Plant Science. After graduation, she moved to Seattle to be closer to her sister. While jogging in the park she met Jeff, an economics professor. He was newly divorced with two children. Ava and Jeff fell in love and they were married in New York by a Justice of the Peace. Secretly, I breathed a sigh of relief that finally my younger daughter had found the stability that had eluded her, as well as love and happiness.

Ava and Jeff moved to Houston, where Charles' shipping company headquarters was located and where we, too, had recently relocated. Jeff went into the family business working with Charles, while Ava began teaching computer science at the University of Houston. They later adopted a beautiful baby girl from China, whom they named Katherine, after me.

Controlling—Me?

"A stunning lady with no reverence for anything or anybody."[5]

"She's a fierce, funny woman, fixing herself to box with the entire world."[6]

When I read those words, I have to acknowledge them. I *have* used control as a defensive weapon for self-protection. As I grew into maturity, other people called the shots and made life decisions for me that I felt were contrary to my better interests. When I eventually reclaimed my life, I became the captain of my own destiny. I found that I liked being in charge and my accomplishments gave me both satisfaction and purpose. (I must say here that I was frequently called the "Dragon Lady" by my nursing colleagues because I was a strict disciplinarian). I needed control over the smallest of details. For example, living in New York, I sewed my family's clothing. I enjoyed the creativity and diversion, but I most enjoyed the sense of power I derived from knowing that I could make the same skirt for five dollars that would cost much more in the store.

I would not be controlled by the domestic limits that I felt were unfairly imposed upon me, and more than once I paid the price. The first time I used a washing machine, I absolutely refused to sort the clothing, as per the directions on the box of detergent. I had to challenge the claims of the soap commercials on TV to see if they were correct or just propaganda. Could the suds clean all the clothing equally well, if the clothing were co-mingled in the washing machine or did they really have to be sorted? Much to my chagrin, and at the cost of my white clothing, I discovered that sometimes directions just needed to followed, and not questioned.

Ambitions Realized
The Bridge Player

How I started playing bridge and how I met my second husband, Charles, are the same story.

I had been married to Chang-Jui for ten years, still a wife, mother, and nurse. My talents as a chef of authentic Chinese cuisine had gained notice, so I often hosted dinner parties for him. During those parties, I would come out briefly to greet our guests and then return to the kitchen. But after serving dinner and cleaning up, I would sit behind the men as they played bridge and discussed the play, or *kibitzed*, their games.

The parties were segregated because the women who came did not speak English well enough to play bridge, and preferred to play the Chinese game of Mah-Jongg. Among the men, bridge was considered a game of the intellectual elite: only the ignorant played Mah-Jongg. "Do you play bridge?" was a code for "How intelligent are you?" If the answer was no, one was considered a 'dum-dum.' I already knew a little bit about bridge because I used to watch my father play with his friends in Chungking, and later in Shanghai. Mother hired a bridge and dance teacher because she believed both skills would enhance our social status. Bridge fascinated me. It was riveting to watch four players argue hand after hand, hurling accusations of "wrong bid" or "wrong play." I could see how they relished the discussion of each hand. "What is it

70

about bridge that makes these successful, powerful men so competitive?" I would wonder.

During one game, Ambassador Liu, the United Nations representative from Taiwan, turned to me. "Would you like to play?" I smiled and shook my head. "Thank you for asking, but I don't really know how to play, I just like to kibitz the game." Chang-Jui cut in on our conversation. "Kathie, don't even try. Women are too emotional and undisciplined to ever learn how to play bridge seriously."

That statement made me angry as hell. I knew he considered women to be inferior, but I was astonished that he would speak so dismissingly of me in front of these esteemed guests. I retorted: "Is that so?? Well, I bet I could learn to play bridge seriously if I tried." Chang-Jui snickered. "Okay, I will bet you five hundred dollars that you cannot master the game of bridge in three months." I quickly accepted.

Making that wager changed my life. Of course I had made Chang-Jui lose face in front of his brother and friends by speaking to him that way. Causing someone to lose face is one of the worse things one can do in Chinese society. I knew that, but I just didn't care anymore. I was fed up with my daily struggle in our hopeless relationship and Chang-Jui's insulting and demeaning attitude toward me.

Over the next two months, I immersed myself in bridge books. I also read *The New York Times*' bridge column daily and talked to a few friends whom I knew played bridge. They all told me that I had made a bad bet—that there was no way one could master bridge in just a quarter of a year. But a bet was a bet, and the clock was ticking. I studied bridge night and day in between working and taking care of my family.

The three months flew by. I telephoned a friend who played bridge quite well and asked him to be my partner. We played in a bridge tournament at the China Institute in New York City, where Charles Wei was the tournament chairman. I would like to say it was love at first sight, but we barely spoke. My bridge partner and I finished third in the tournament. I won my bet and my freedom from Chang-Jui. So, in a way, this game of cards 'bridged' the gap between my life with Chang-Jui and my life with Charles.

C.C. Wei

My first bridge tournament was a life-changing event for me for more than one reason. Not only did I begin the path that would bring me to fame and success, I also met the man who would guide and accompany me along this path. Charles (C.C.) Wei was my second husband, my soul mate.

Charles was a well-known Chinese-American shipping entrepreneur. He had been director of the first tournament I'd attended. It was a small six-table event with only 12 teams but we spoke only briefly. I later heard from a friend that C.C. Wei had asked about me. "Who is that attractive woman?" My friend replied, "Forget it. She's married with three children."

Ambitions Realized: The Bridge Player

The next time we met was a chance encounter at a combination bridge and mah-jongg party sponsored by the consul general's office and hosted by Madame Chiang, wife of President Chiang Kai-shek. This was in the late 1960s. Chang-Jui and I had been invited to the gathering, but he was in Europe at the time, and we'd been separated for some time. I went alone. Toward the end of the evening, I needed a ride, and someone suggested that one of the gentleman guests, C.C. Wei, drive me home.

On the way home, his car broke down, and, to his great surprise, I was able to fix it. That must have really impressed him, because he wanted to get together again. We started dating after a few casual meetings. Charles was also separated from his wife, so we didn't tell our children of our budding relationship. Divorce was not acceptable in Chinese society—we needed to be discreet.

After dating for a while, we both knew we were in love. We married in 1968, after our divorces were final. I did not feel like this was a *second* marriage: Charles made me feel like a cherished bride. Throughout our marriage, he treated me like I was the most beautiful woman in the world.

We were married by a judge in New York's City Hall. The reception was held at the JFK Airport hotel, given by my bosses Dr. Starr and Dr. Abelson. Charles and I did not invite any of our children, fearing their disapproval. The decision not to include them was a big mistake, one that I regret to this day. I was selfish and insensitive, but I was happy, in love, and was loved in return.

We lived in New York part-time and the rest of the time in Houston, site of the business offices for Charles' shipping business. His Chinese name was Chung-Ching Wei, known to many people as C.C. Wei, but I preferred to call him Charles. He was a phenomenon, a man with vision. He made his name in the field of shipping, but used his influence with humanitarian goals in mind. In those days, for example, acupuncture wasn't respected as a medical treatment. Charles tried to make acupuncture accessible for those who needed it. He set up a research foundation to explain and promote its benefits.

Charles loved his life and I loved sharing it with him. He infused our lives with excitement and fun. My daughter Ada remembers Charles as "an extraordinary step-father... a brilliant engineer, businessman and ship-builder."[7] He was a well-known entrepreneur, and as such we attended political and charitable functions where we were on a first-name basis with many congressional leaders. Presidents Ronald Reagan and George Bush invited us to the White House. When Chinese leaders came to Washington, these presidents would seek our advice on matters related to Chinese culture and politics. It was exhilarating!

Ambitions Realized

"Ambitions come in two varieties—sternly realistic and hopelessly remote...

Once upon a time, about 15 years ago, there were two New Yorkers with ambitions of the second kind. One was a busy ship owner with an interest in bridge theory but with no practical experience who wanted to create a popular bidding system—one that would perhaps win two different World titles in a single day. His chances were just about nil, since in the history of the game no non-expert had ever created an effective system and persuaded the experts to use it.

The second New Yorker was a woman who had worked hard for many years as a nurse as well as bringing up a family. She had just learned bridge, was intrigued by it, and thought she would like to become a world champion. She stood, however, little chance, inasmuch as nobody who started playing when past college age had ever won a World title.

Shortly after, these two got married, having in common their interest in the game, strong drives in slightly different directions and a birthplace in mainland China…

Three weeks ago in New Orleans…it all came true in a parley that no fiction writer would dare to suggest. Kathie Wei won the World Women's Pair championship… and she was using the precision system invented by her husband, Charles Wei…"

— "Ambitions Realized" by Alan Truscott, *The New York Times,* July, 1978.

The 1978 World Bridge Federation Olympiad where Kathie won a gold medal in New Orleans.

In bridge, your objective is to use a system of bidding to describe your unseen hand to your partner. This is not easy to do, and you must rely on judgment, reasoning, logic, and creativity, in order to be successful. You attempt to utilize a bridge language to communicate effectively with your partner. Many different bidding systems have been invented. Some are better than others.

An engineer by training, Charles spent many years analyzing the strengths and weakness of many of these bidding languages or systems. He also discovered why they were ineffective. His invention of the Precision bidding system addressed and solved many of the problems associated with traditional or standard bidding systems. More specifically, he designed Precision to facilitate communication with one's partner, and, at the same time, to make communication between the opponents difficult. Precision is a logical, creative, and effective system.

Ironically, while Charles played bridge, he wasn't an expert or even an especially strong player. He didn't really like participating in bridge tournaments. He would say that playing in a tournament was like taking a test and being graded on it, which he hated. I, too, hadn't had any significant successes at the bridge table before Precision. I didn't play bridge until my 30s. As a comparison, players now who aspire to the top levels of bridge start playing and studying the game while still in their teens.

So Charles invented Precision and I used and promoted the system. There was a rumor that Charles invented the Precision system as a gift for me, but that's not accurate. He had created the system before we had ever met. Charles taught my bridge partners and me how to succeed at Precision. He created hundreds of specific hands so we could practice normal bidding situations, as well as more unusual hands. We discussed and analyzed problems that we faced using Precision. Modifications were made when necessary. We spent months and months learning the system.

Initially, Precision didn't attract much attention in the bridge community. But that changed when the Taiwan national team, using Precision, finished second in the 1969 Bermuda Bowl world championship ahead of a strong third-place North American team. Charles and I then co-captained the Chinese team in the World Championships in Rio in 1969, and when the team did better than anyone had expected, finishing second to a powerful Italian team, I became hooked on bridge and on Precision.

I promoted Precision by travelling around the world teaching and coaching bridge teams that went on to win world titles, specifically the Chinese, Chinese-Taipei, and Israeli teams. In the early 1970s, Charles sponsored a team of young experts who had a number of successes in U. S. competition playing Precision.

Since then, Precision has been used successfully by many international teams on the world stage in bridge. Even with the advent of new bidding systems, Precision remains an accurate, structured means of effective communication with one's partner.

Falcon Shipping Company

Charles was an engineer by training, and got his start in the industry during World War II as a radio engineer working with ships and ground transportation in China. In 1942 he was sent to the U.S. to work for Chiang Kai-shek's government. He launched his shipping career when he helped to get oil from the Middle East for an embattled Taiwan. When the war ended, he remained in the U.S. and married a woman from Shanghai. He had two children, a boy and a girl. He managed a U.S. shipping firm until 1960, when he became an independent owner.

Charles formed a business partnership with Houston Wasson, a successful entrepreneur; their enterprise, the Falcon Shipping Group, lasted more than four decades. They had headquarters in Houston and offices in New York, Nashville, and Boca Raton. The company had a fleet of 17 American flag tankers and bulk carriers, most of which served the U.S. Navy's Military Sealift Command. Their ships flew the American flag, affording jobs and good pay to American mariners. After World War II, many ship owners discarded the U.S. flag in favor of sailing under foreign flags that were subject to less regulation and that permitted the hiring of cheaper labor. Charles and Houston wanted to revitalize the United States Merchant Marine, and provide fast and efficient shipping vessels that would challenge foreign competition.

After our divorces, Charles and I married in 1968. He asked me to consider working with him at Falcon, which would mean retiring from my career in nursing.

C.C. Wei

I had just won my first gold medal in bridge in New Orleans in 1978. I attributed that win to beginner's luck. I saw bridge more as a pastime than a career. I gave it some thought before joining Charles at Falcon.

My first job title at Falcon was Social Director, a demanding and stressful position. I was responsible for getting the right people to attend shipping launches, organizing receptions, and promoting events with the media. Each detail was important, even which CEO's wife disliked a particular color.

As a lobbyist for the Merchant Marines, I traveled to Washington every other week to promote the U.S. flag shipping business. At the time, my name was also becoming recognized as a bridge champion, and whenever bridge-playing senators or congressmen heard I was in town, they'd track me down to play some bridge! Justice John Paul Stevens, a recent Ford appointee to the Supreme Court, was a fan, and I always had time to sit down and play a few hands with him. But my primary mission was to secure opportunities for U.S. flag merchant ships. I wrote to then-President Reagan:

"The U.S. maritime industry has made great strides in making our transportation services as competitive as possible in the world market place. It was C.C. Wei who revolutionized American shipping by developing new diesel-propelled tankers and bulk carriers. He led the effort to drastically reduce manning levels and wage scales to make American ships more competitive. All we ask from the government is assistance in the form of realistic maritime promotion programs to ensure equity and fairness in global markets."

Charles was always dreaming up new ventures. He wanted to buy a fishery in Kodiak, Alaska, which would diversify our business. We could add many fishing vessels to our fleet, so we became fully invested in this enterprise as well.

When I joined the company, I was a woman in a man's world. Men were not accustomed to taking orders from a woman, even if it was the wife of its founder and co-owner. My credibility and authority were tested constantly. I had to demonstrate to our employees that I got my job due to merit, perseverance, and my industrious nature. Part of my success was due to the fact that I didn't talk down to my employees, and I never asked anyone to do something I would not do. I believed that things would ultimately improve for women in the workplace, but at that time it was extremely difficult.

Kathie, seen here on the right, joined other business and political officials in celebrating the first commercial bulk vessel flying the U.S. flag in more than 50 years

After a few years, I was promoted to Senior VP. In 1981, I assisted negotiations for the first Sino-American grain agreement. I joined Chinese officials in Beijing in welcoming our *Pride of Texas,* the first bulk vessel in more than 50 years, flying the American flag while transporting grain to China. A mutual interest in bridge led to connections with the then Chinese Vice-Premier Deng Xiaoping and participation in trade agreements between the U.S. and China.

Because of my recognition as an international

bridge player, business links with China, and knowledge of Chinese customs and language, I received an invitation to the White House to advise President Reagan on Chinese culture and affairs for his upcoming trip to Beijing.

The President kept stumbling over the official name for China. He confused the People's Repub-

Kathie with President Ronald Reagan

lic of China (the PRC), referring to mainland China, with the Republic of China (the ROC), which is Taiwan. I said, "Mr. President, if you use the wrong term, your hosts will be insulted. Be better to just say "China."

In Washington I also met with business leaders who shared with me their concerns about why they were uncomfortable pursuing trade with China. The failures of the economic policies of the Great Leap Forward in the late '50s and the political excesses of Mao's Cultural Revolution in the late '60s, had made American businesses reluctant to invest in China. I expressed my belief that the Chinese had learned from this folly and would not regress. Deng Xiaoping helped to modernize China by retiring the veterans of the Red Guard and replacing them with better educated, forward-thinking members of a younger generation. But I also cautioned the U.S. business community against regarding China as a lesser power. China, no longer the colonial state occupied by Western powers and Imperial Japan, wanted to be respected as equals. China represented the future of trade. It was in the best interests of American businesses to acknowledge this fact.

I returned from my eye-opening adventures in Washington to Falcon. By 1984, I was doing all the business travel for our shipping company. I was in Israel meeting with the shipyard people in Haifa to do some dry-dock repair on one of our ships, when I received news that Charles had been admitted to a New York hospital. His illness had plagued him for

In the Congressional Record, North Carolina Rep. Walter Jones referred to C.C. Wei as a "brilliant businessman."

years, but nothing could prepare me for his death.

Walter B. Jones, congressman of North Carolina, paid tribute to Charles in the Congressional Record of the 100th Congress. He listed his many accomplishments, hailing him as "... a brilliant businessman who wisely challenged the mistaken notion that commitment to U.S. flag shipping cannot be profitable for both labor and management. He found American flag cargo opportunities where few believed they existed... (he) was an innovator, an entrepreneur, and in many ways, a pioneer like those who founded and built the country he adopted, and which adopted him."[8]

Losing Charles

Charles died suddenly, but his death was not sudden. When I returned, we had only a few remaining years together. For five of those last years, Charles suffered from diabetes and liver disease, complicated by severe infections.

As we were leaving the hospital after one of his many transfusions, Charles said to me "Kathie, I don't intend to die for a long time—but if I do, I want you to know that our life together needs to be celebrated. Make my funeral a happy one! I want you to read the poem "No Funeral Gloom," by William Allingham.

I tried to make light of this. "You promised me 40 years together. Who knows, maybe you'll come up with an even better poem before that!" We went home and Charles lived for another year. We never discussed death again. He returned to the hospital many times, and endured countless blood transfusions and intravenous antibiotics. He lived and dealt with his illness with optimism. He gave me the best of himself, as well as he could. In Chinese custom it is considered bad luck to even think or talk about death—no one wants to confront death head on.

Charles' condition degenerated to the point where he entered the hospital for a final visit. I refused to accept that he was dying. I sat vigil by his bedside, stroking his hair and arms, kissing him whenever he opened his eyes. On a cold winter's day in February, 1987, he opened his eyes one final time, smiled at me and stopped breathing. He was only 71 years old.

For three years, both Charles and I never accepted the fact that he was near death. I felt stupid and cowardly. I'd been so selfish in continuing to live my life without preparing for the end. At times I hated him for dying and leaving me behind, but most days I just grieved. I missed him impossibly. Suddenly alone, and aching with sadness, I found myself unable to deal with his leaving me and all the incomplete issues and details associated with our life and business together.

Most of all, I was upset with God for taking my dearest love. Charles had believed in God, but not in organized religion. I'd tried to convince him to become a Baptist, but he had refused. He said, "God is constant in my heart, and when you are a good person and do good deeds to help other human beings, God will be there for you." When he died, I became disillusioned with God. Charles didn't keep his promise to me not to die, nor did God reward him for being a good person. I stopped believing in God after Charles' death. I thought He was indifferent or deliberately neglectful toward me. I even started reflecting on the purpose of my own life now. Why would I want to live after Charles' death?

At the funeral, Charles' coffin was covered with the elegant white orchids and lilies that he had requested to adorn a simple casket. Friends and family were there to help lessen my pain and grief.

From a distance, my young friend Anton Li played Charles' favorite melodies on his violin, including Louis Armstrong's "What a Wonderful World." The soft, doleful lyrics, "I see skies of blue and clouds of white... and I think to myself what a wonderful world" did little to comfort my aching soul. Anton also played Jascha Heifetz's adaptation of Mendelssohn's "Sweet Remembrance" and the mournful Chinese songs I'd chosen to offer my final goodbyes.

Over fifty cars accompanied us to Pine Lawn Cemetery. It took almost an hour traveling along the busy Long Island Expressway. In the past, I always dreaded the traffic along this route, but now I was hoping that the ride would never end, that I could ride forever with Charles. When the limousine stopped suddenly, waking me from my thoughts, I had to come to the terms of our final trip together. Ada and Ava helped me as I struggled to get out of the car. We walked slowly toward Charles' coffin, which had been placed on the earth next to a big empty space in the ground. I glanced around the cemetery. Fountains and shadowy trees seemed to be standing watch over the headstones. The grey skies had opened, quietly releasing heavy snowflakes. I realized that I would be leaving my Charles here forever.

"Ada," I said, "This can't be true. This can't really be happening. Charles can't be dead. He promised me he wouldn't die before me."

"Mom, remember your promise to Uncle Charles. You need to celebrate his life. You can't let him down now," Ada whispered. Ava handed me another tissue.

I could hear Charles' voice. "No tears or sadness for me when I die. Just remember all the happy years we had together. After all, we already overdrew our happiness account." I forced myself to stand up straight. I wiped away my tears and dug into my coat pocket for William Allingham's poem.

> No funeral gloom, my dears, when I
> am gone,
> corpse-gazing, tears, black raiment,
> graveyard grimness.
> Think of me as withdrawn into the
> dimness,
> yours still, you mine.
> Remember all the best of our past
> moments,
> and forget the rest;
> and so to where I wait,
> come gently on.

Somewhere, I knew that Charles would hear me reading.

Hundreds of guests—family and friends—came to the party I'd arranged at Charles' insistence. We raised our glasses to toast an extraordinary human being and extremely successful businessman, a man of brilliance who showed me that nothing was impossible. He gave me much love and courage, and taught me that we are living in a wonderful world. The guests who spoke shared their experiences; business associates and friends, bridge-world friends, and friends from Chinese society all revealed to me more than I had ever known of Charles' generosity and compassion. I smiled and drew comfort as they praised him.

Memories of my mother, however, were anything but comforting. I began to have nightmares about her. She would point her finger at me and say in a voice full of judgment, "I knew you were going to have troubles, because you didn't listen to me. You gave up on the marriage that I had arranged for you."

In these dreams I would respond, "But Mother, I gave him two daughters. And a son! I continued with my education and was successful in my different careers. But I was so unhappy in that marriage. His controlling ways smothered me. I couldn't grow into the person I wanted to be."

She would continue her tirade. "No! You divorced him to marry that C.C. Wei. You're unhappy because you refused to be a good Chinese wife to Chang-Jui. He even gave you a son! You never should have left him. Look, C.C. Wei left you, too."

"No, Mother," I'd whisper. "He didn't leave me. He died."

Her face would turn beet-red and she'd shout me down. "No! That was God's way of punishing you for breaking your marriage vows!"

I couldn't escape these recurring nightly visits.

The anguish of Charles' passing took its toll.

One bleak day, shortly after his funeral, all my children and friends finally went home. I was alone, and sat by the window of our 32nd-floor apartment on the East Side of Manhattan, looking out at the United Nations. I regarded that distant building and the East River, and suddenly considered jumping out the window, onto the street of the city I adored. It would not just end it all—no more torment, no unendurable suffering—but it would be a way to be with Charles again. I had never thought of taking my own life before; this was not who I was. But I saw no point in living without love and the one person to whom I'd committed my whole being.

Shaking, I opened the window and resolutely stuck my head out. The icy wind sheared my cheeks. My heart pounded as I looked down at the street below. Then, distantly, I could hear Charles' voice.

"Don't do this to yourself. Don't do this to your children and don't do this to me."

The sound of an airplane flying above the skyline shook me alive. I ran to my medicine cabinet and dumped a bottle of anti-depressants in the toilet, ashamed that I could have such thoughts. I grabbed one of Charles' photos and held it close to me, sobbing until I fell asleep. When I woke, I realized that in order to continue living, I had to acknowledge death. Charles was gone.

I continued working in our business, and was elected chairman of the Falcon Shipping Group and the Alaskan Fishery. On March 24, 1989, things started to fail. The Exxon Valdez, an oil tanker owned by the Exxon Shipping Company, spilled 11 million gallons of crude oil into Alaska's Prince William Sound. It was, at that time, the worst oil spill in U.S. history, devastating the fishing industry. Fishermen went bankrupt, and the economies of shoreline towns suffered in the following years. To cut their losses, local fishermen went over to help the Exxon cleanup. Week after week, we had no fish to process. Our factory soon ran out of money and we were forced to close, leaving many people in Alaska without jobs. Houston Wasson, co-owner of the Falcon Shipping Group, and I flew to Alaska to sign the closing documents.

Another year went by. The Cold War was ending. Defense industries were hit especially hard, as was the shipping industry. It was time for me to retire. Houston and I closed our shipping company. It was a sad day for me and it was the end of a great era for C.C. Wei.

The world Charles opened to me was exciting and rich with purpose. In our partnership, he had all the great ideas and I was his instrument who carried them out. I miss his love and support, forward-thinking ideas, as well as his ability to create new ideas and forge them into reality.

Fortunately, my interest in bridge spared me from severe depression. Later, armed with years of experience and worldly connections, I was able to start my own consulting company with great success. Bridge was the buoy that supported me.

Return to China

For more than thirty years I'd had no direct communication with my parents. Alice would send brief, polite notes, summarizing family news and thanking me for the gifts of money I'd sent them. I'd not heard from either of my parents directly, even when we wrote to tell them of the births of grand-children.

What I was not totally aware of was the degree to which my family had been affected by "The Great Terror." The decades following the communist takeover of China saw unspeakable horrors. Books had been burned, museums destroyed, and ancient cultural artifacts smashed. Traditional Chinese culture had flourished for thousands of years, and the communist regime destroyed it.

Anyone who didn't agree with the new autocratic government was regarded as an enemy of the state. This included not only members of the losing side of the civil war under Chiang Kai-shek, but also many ordinary citizens, students, teachers, and scholars. Since these people held old beliefs, the new regime felt they could not be trusted to support and further the communist party line. Many were sent to reeducation camps to think 'correctly.' Many were tortured or killed. Members of my own family were sent to be reeducated. They returned as irreparably damaged human beings.

In the fall of 1981, after three decades, I returned home to Hankow in Wuhan. My father was dying. Through contacts in Hong Kong and Taiwan, I had learned about my family's state of affairs. I finally received a single letter in my father's spidery but still elegant calligraphy. "You must come now to our home in Hankow. It's shameful for a parent to have to beg not to be neglected by his child, but I am going to die soon, and I want to see my second daughter, who judging from what her dutiful sister tells us, has flourished so in the West."

Kathie returned to Wuhan after not seeing her family for 32 years.

The handwriting was so familiar—but so was the tone. This letter had clearly been Mother's work. With the sorrowful news also came with a list of Western commodities that she commanded me to buy for her. "Bring all the items listed below," she had dictated. "Our commune leader has made inquiries on our behalf. A portion of the 100% import tax will be waived."

My sisters explained to me that our parents lived in what was considered an excellent commune and that their apartment was the finest in that area. To get there, I walked down a dark, smoky alley in which there were eight one-room family dwellings. At one end of the alley stood an outhouse, at the other end a stove and two water faucets. The facilities were shared by all eight families. I was appalled by these 'fine' conditions. The small, square room had only a few wooden chairs and two beds. A corner of the room had a drainage grate; water brought from outside provided the only means for washing. The floor was made of cement. Yet packed incongruously into this tiny residence were all of the appliances and gadgets I'd sent over the years, including the items on the newest list. We could barely move around.

As I entered the tiny apartment, Mother accosted me with shrieks and wails. The events of the last thirty-two years had aged her, but her face was still smooth and unlined. She'd recently had a hip operation and was confined to her bed. She seemed a shrunken version of the person I'd left.

She refused to talk to me about the years we'd lived apart. I had found out from relatives the tragic story of my sister Alice: her fiancé, of whom mother and father had never approved, fled to France the month after Shanghai fell, in order to escape a violent

After not seeing her birth family in China for 32 years, Kathie flew to China in the fall of 1981 to see them.

racial purity movement. Mother quickly found Alice a husband, who abandoned her three months before she gave birth to an illegitimate child. She was publicly shamed on the streets of Shanghai and was sent away by the government to the countryside.

Father was sentenced to four harsh years in a labor camp for being a 'reactionary' and 'intellectual.' His health had suffered greatly and my heart crumpled when I saw him. My once-spirited and robust father looked fragile, a shell of his former self. This esteemed scholar had been relegated to an insulting and lowly position by the communist regime—he was a clerk in the library he once directed. Previously, he had been forced to work as a street cleaner and wear a sign around his neck that read "Capitalist sympathizer," because his daughter lived in the U.S.

Father had prostate cancer. The day I arrived, his bladder was painfully distended, and his tongue was so swollen that he couldn't speak. His pallor was an awful yellow-gray. He lay on a plank of wood covered with a mattress of thin cotton and I sat with him and spoke to him quietly about the things I knew he'd want to hear: his grandchildren, my husband, my career as a nurse. He squeezed my hand, unable to communicate, but he was with me. I hated to see his torment. After three unbearable days, I convinced Party officials to admit him to the hospital.

As he lay dying in his hospital room, mother entertained the friends who came to visit. She showed them Polaroid pictures of all the gifts I'd brought from the U.S., and showed me off as the Western oddity I was. They chattered away. I couldn't wait for them to leave.

I was an experienced nurse, and I knew that my father was in great pain. The hospital could not help him. His condition was terminal. I knew that Father would not want to end his life this way. After consultation with his doctors, I made the decision to end Father's life-support. My sister Joan agreed with me, but my older sister Alice and third sister Victoria would not talk to me or forgive me for years after-ward. I knew that I had done the right thing for our father. He did not need to suffer any longer.

During this time, Mother would discuss none of her life under the communist regime with me. "It's not permitted," she whispered, telling me to keep my voice down. She was afraid that her neighbor, the commune's leader, would overhear the conversation, and report us.

"Mother," I whispered, "why don't we talk, just you and I?"

No answer. She sat with her back to me, lost in herself.

"Mother?" I repeated.

"Not now, Katherine."

Even now, I wished things could have been different between us. We were mother and daughter, but bound only by our genes. Nothing had changed from when I was young. We weren't able to communicate meaningfully with one another. The few words that mother did utter were critical of my life decisions, my personality, and the adult I had become. She was still quite good at heaping blame. Her questions about my life in America were vague and general; she showed no interest in what I had become. It was as if she didn't want to be burdened by anything I had to share with her. Her cruel remarks had always been painful, but at least she had been talking to me. It was her silence that I couldn't endure.

Although she and I were so different, I had inherited her drive to succeed, strength of will, outspoken character. But even this was a mixed blessing. Professionally, I felt such pride in my ability to assist critically ill patients as a nurse. But I had pushed myself too hard, working overtime and neglecting my children. Often, during the years of raising my children, I'd catch myself making the same mistakes my mother had made with my sisters and me. To this day, I feel that I need approval from my friends as a substitute for mother's withheld love.

"I guess things won't ever change between us, will they Mother?" I asked one last time.

Her response was slow in coming.

"I suppose not."

Father died within the week, and Mother less than a year later. My memories are not of a father's dying look of love for his daughter, but my mother's hint of a smile, her impenetrable gaze.

Perhaps Mother and I had both been released.

Starting Over with Henry

The first time Henry Sender saw me, it was love at first sight—for him. "Struck by lightning," was how he put it. We were both in the American Airlines Admiral lounge sometime in May of 1990. I was sitting in a chair yoga style, knitting and listening to music through my headphones. He told me later he'd thought, "I would really like to meet this beautiful lady." As it turned out, we were both going to Tennessee on the same flight. Henry was flying to Nashville, while I was going to Memphis via Nashville to attend a bridge tournament. Coincidentally, I was sitting in seat 7A and Henry was sitting right next to me in 7B. Henry would call that *bashert*; I might call it *yuan-fen*. In any language, it was fate.

The weather was perfect that day, clear and cloudless. As our plane took off from LaGuardia to Nashville, I was gazing out at the steely skyscrapers shrinking in the distance. I turned to my right and looked directly at Henry. I do not know, to this day, what made me start a conversation with a stranger.

"My lucky day! What a handsome traveling companion," I gushed.

He looked at me in surprise, and his expression brightened. He smiled and extended a firm handshake, saying, "Henry Sender, Nashville, Tennessee. It is I who am the lucky one to have **you** sitting next to me."

I smiled back and gave him a less steady hand.

"Kathie Wei, New York City."

Henry told me that he was usually upgraded to
first class but it was his good fortune that he didn't
this time, as he got to sit next to me. We chatted
for a while, and then Henry told me that he was in
mourning. His 34-year-old son had died, and following their son's death, Henry's wife had committed suicide in the bed they had shared for forty-two
years. I was taken aback that someone would reveal
such intimate details to a total stranger. But maybe
a stranger was what he needed to speak so frankly.

"How did your son die?" I asked.

Henry shook his head sadly. "He was a talented architect working in South Beach, Florida. He
fell off a building on the job and was pronounced
dead at the scene."

The loss of any son would be devastating,
but I learned that Henry and Randy had been best
friends. They shared many interests; in fact, they
were both architects. Randy's death would affect
Henry for the rest of his life. On the deepest level
I could empathize. I offered my story of Charles'
passing, and how lost I too, had felt. We talked.
We sighed. We talked some more. I didn't want the
remainder of our trip to be so morbid, so I changed
the subject.

"Where were you during World War II?"

"I was born in Strasbourg, the capital of Alsace-Lorraine, which borders France and Germany.
I fled to the U.S. because of the Nazi invasion, and
enlisted in the U.S. Army as soon as I turned eigh-

teen. Since I spoke German and French, the army put me in the counter-intelligence corps attached to the Office of Strategic Services."

"Does that mean you were a spy?"

Henry chuckled. "One might say so. We parachuted into Normandy twenty-seven days before D-Day. We landed in uncertain territory but when I saw a flashlight in my face instead of a gun, I knew we were in the right place. We later made contact with the French Freedom Fighters."

"Was it frightening jumping out of an airplane?"

"We were nervous, but not scared. I guess our youth helped us at the time. We carried a lot of weapons, and printed inside our leather jackets was a map of Europe as well as the special words: I am not a spy."

Hearing Henry's story I was getting a vastly different perspective on the war I too had experienced. In *my* war, Japanese Imperial forces had committed the atrocities, but I was a civilian. I hadn't fought for my freedom—at least not with weapons.

Our plane was about to land in Nashville. I did not want our conversation to end. I asked Henry about his experiences in Europe, how it felt to be part of the forces that defeated the evil of Hitler and his Nazis. With an impish smile, he replied, "This story takes a long time. I would need to come to New York at least once a week to tell it all to you!"

I can't say that it was love at first sight for me.

But Henry had definitely sparked something, and I wanted to see him again. On the surface, we didn't seem a likely pair—I wasn't Caucasian, didn't share his religion, and I was no spring chicken— over 50 years old. But something told me that I needed to hear more about the invasion of Normandy, and I needed to hear it from him.

Kathie and Henry

True to his word, Henry came to New York. He had wonderful taste in restaurants and shows, and we took advantage of New York's cultural riches. He shared more of his life with me, and I gave him a copy of my book, *Second Daughter,* so he could understand my life as a young girl in China. He was a great storyteller. I loved to hear him talk about his experiences during World War II. And what a courtly Southern gentleman he was! I began to think that drawing seat numbers 7A and 7B on that Nashville-bound flight was like winning the lottery.

Although Henry came weekly to visit me from Tennessee, I would not let him come up to my apartment for four months. Much later in our relationship, Henry would say, "When Kathie wouldn't let me go up to her condominium, I thought I'd lost it all." He was just becoming acquainted with my willful character.

Henry saw from our first meeting that I could be bold, and as we spent more time together, he saw that I rarely hesitated in expressing my opinions. My fearlessness and willingness to embark on new adventures intrigued him, but he was not accustomed to these characteristics in a woman. He struggled to accept such strength in a possible wife. Later on, after we'd been married for a while, he'd say, "The woman is capable of doing anything she puts her mind to. I wouldn't dare her on anything."

Starting Over with Henry

We had an unusual relationship. I was a Chinese-American woman twice married, a Democrat in my late fifties, and he was a Jewish immigrant from Europe in his sixties, a Republican. Nevertheless, I found myself falling in love with Henry. When he asked me to marry him, my response should have been obvious—and immediate. But I was wracked with guilt about loving a man who wasn't Charles.

I didn't know what to do. I was almost 60—could I start over? After two marriages, I didn't think that I could have feelings for another man. Would I be betraying my second husband by loving someone else? Could I keep the memory of his love intact? Also, could I live with someone daily who felt his own losses so acutely?

On the other hand, should I close the book on new love and romance?

I woke up one day and looked out my window. The rainy, gloomy New York morning was like a dirty mirror reflecting my soul. I felt old and used up. I realized then that Henry was the tonic I needed to restore my vitality, my future. Maybe this was *beshert*—my destiny. But first I needed Charles' permission to marry someone else. I needed the spiritual release from Charles and his memory that would free me to love and live with Henry in the present.

I traveled to Long Island alone to visit Charles' grave. The bright, sunny day contrasted with the heavy winter sky the day of his funeral. The forlorn trees standing sentinel over the graves were now in bloom, encouraging my visit. I found Charles' grave and saw that his name was inscribed both in English and Chinese. "Wei Chungking, A life of a great man stopped by death."

I had brought white orchids and gently placed them on his grave. I touched his name on the gravestone and felt his presence there. I started to call him by name, first in English and then in Chinese. I told him all about Henry. I told him that I could be happy with Henry, that we shared both personal tragedies and the promise of a good life together.

I asked him for his blessings and permission to marry Henry, and then sat for a long time waiting for an answer. The sun was setting as the leaves softly rustled around me. I can't be sure, but I think I heard Charles murmur his assent.

With my acceptance of Henry's marriage proposal came the issue of religion. Although I was a non-practicing Baptist, Henry was Jewish, and his religion was extremely important to him. He had been the last *bar-mitzvah* at his synagogue in Alsace-Lorraine before it was burned to the ground by the Nazis the following year. Henry and his father escaped to the United States in 1938 but most of his friends and family perished in the Holocaust.

Henry wanted to take an active part in defending his adopted country's fight for freedom. At 17, he tried to enlist in the U.S. Army but was not accepted until the following year, 1943, when he became both soldier and an American citizen. His multilingual abilities made him a natural choice to work with the free French forces, and to capture and interrogate spies.

Ten months before the end of the war, Henry was made commander of his unit. He was assigned to a location that was close to the town where his mother had been buried. Determined to visit his mother's grave, Henry took his jeep and loaded it with an arsenal of weapons. As he entered the town, he noticed a number of white sheets hanging from some of the windows. He was puzzled at first, until he realized that the town was surrendering to him. Henry captured the town without firing a shot. The *burgermeister* approached him with the key to the city, a gesture that represented his surrender to the U.S.

Henry accepted the surrender and told the mayor that he wanted to visit the cemetery where his mother had been buried. The small Jewish cemetery on the outskirts of the village looked like its own war zone. Headstones were overturned and lay in the dirt like fallen soldiers. Some were uprooted and broken in half. Henry returned to the *burgermeister* in a rage. "Either you restore this cemetery to its former dignity," he uttered in perfect German, "Or there will be many of your townspeople occupying *other* cemeteries!" The mayor hastily complied.

Just as he took great pride in being American and Jewish, Henry was so proud of this accomplishment. His stories showed me what his faith meant to him, so when he asked me to convert to Judaism, I agreed. I said "yes" to the whole package: moving to Nashville, living a Southern way of life, and establishing a traditional Jewish household. I figured—I'd conquered New York! I'd played bridge with world leaders! I'd even made peace with a washing machine! How difficult could *this be?*

Changes

"One of the world's best-known bridge personalities changed her name yesterday, and thousands of her friends will have to get used to it. Kathie Wei was married in Seattle to Henry Sender, and will live in Nashville. In preparation for this step, she became a convert to Judaism a month ago. Marriage will not, however, slow down her bridge activity: later this month she will be in China, competing in several tournaments."

—Alan Truscott, *The New York Times*
January 9, 1993

In October 1992, I began my one-year journey into the heart of what it means to be a traditional Jewish woman. The conversion process involved serious immersion in Judaic studies, as well as courses in holidays, prayers, and history and culture. I was given a book called *For Love of Torah*, in which I found a particularly reassuring passage:

Equal law for all.
You shall have one manner of law
for the stranger as for the native-born.

You shall love the stranger,
for you were strangers in
the land of Egypt.

For I am the Lord your God.

Reading this, I felt that my 'otherness' was inconsequential: in Judaism, I could be both accepted and welcomed as an equal.

It was a wonderful and enlightening year. I traveled back and forth to New York to visit friends who helped me with my studies. I learned about the observance of Yom Kippur, the Day of Atonement, and was particularly moved by the notion of being inscribed in the *Book of Life*. Singing the "Sh'ma Yisrael," the prayer that affirms God's covenant with the Jewish people, instilled in me a sense of peace and belonging. As I completed my studies, we selected my Hebrew name, Rachel. The biblical significance of being a second (in this case, third) wife was not lost on me.

We married in 1993, at the beautiful Mercer Island Synagogue in Seattle. As a new convert, I was concerned I would not recall all the wedding vows and blessings in Hebrew. I was a nervous actress, afraid of forgetting the script—and these lines really counted!

Our wedding was a special event for both of us, and was attended by children, grandchildren and best friends. Our union was consecrated under a *chuppah* by three rabbis—all of whom had played significant roles in Henry's life. All three of my children participated in this wedding. I felt complete.

Henry held my hand in his as we left the synagogue, husband and wife. A notion took me suddenly. "What would my mother think of this wedding?" I was in my sixties and still concerned about winning her approval. Mother had long since passed away, but I couldn't help myself.

After the wedding, Henry and I traveled to China on business. We went to Beijing, Shanghai, Chungking, and Hong Kong. We honeymooned in Israel where Henry attended meetings on behalf of the Conservative Jewish Movement while I attended the Israel Bridge Festival in Tel Aviv. I took great pride in attending as a Jewish bridge player. Several months later, at a tournament in Seattle, one of my opponents commented on a risky play I'd made, for which I'd received an extra trick.

"Only Jewish people would make a play like that," said the gentleman, obviously including himself in the flattering comment. I said nothing, but reached into my blouse and pulled out a chain with my Star of David.

When we returned to the U.S., I moved into Henry's house in Belle Meade, just outside Nashville, and Henry helped me close down my office and apartments in New York and Houston. I had lived in New York most of my adult life. Becoming a Southerner would not be easy. A further challenge was adapting to my new residence, the house in which Henry had shared a life with his late wife. Her presence was everywhere.

To his credit, and my great relief, Henry agreed to renovate the house he had built for his wife and family. He gave me free rein to re-create a place where the two of us would start our lives together. The result of my desires and his architectural ingenuity was a spacious, open dwelling, with expansive walls where I could hang my Qing Dynasty tapestry and Chinese paintings. We retained one part of the original house, the brick walls and the fireplaces, so that Henry could display his collection of *shofars*. Picture windows opened onto a yard that hosted many varieties of trees, including dogwoods and Japanese dwarf maples, and the bamboo tree and delicate willow both connected me to my childhood in China. Lin Yutang, the Chinese novelist, calls windows "an unintentional painting." We spent many hours gazing through our natural gallery.

Loss

Henry and I were married for 27 wonderful years. We shared the goodness in our lives and helped each other through the trials of our personal losses. Henry suffered periods of abject sadness.

I had learned about the death of Henry's son the first time I met him, his tragic fall from a building while he was on the job. Randy had everything going for him: he was bright, good looking, with a master's degree in architecture. At age 34, he was already well known in the Miami area as the king of the avant-garde movement. The historic renovations and preservations around the beach were his, and one can't walk around Miami without seeing Randy's architectural work to this day. It was only many years later that I came to learn that the events surrounding Randy's death were not clear. Some family members thought he suffered from depression and that he deliberately jumped. Mental illness seemed to run in the family— Randy's mother also committed suicide.

I offered comfort by reassuring Henry that his wife and son were at peace together. I hoped that Charles was somewhere with them as well. Together, we found a way to make each other embrace and enjoy life in our twilight.

My Buddhist friends say there is a ritual where if a person makes a burnt offering of food, money, or a message, their loved one will receive it in heaven. Before each Chinese holiday they would ask me if I would like to send something to Charles. One year I wrote a letter to Charles to introduce Henry's Polly and Randy to him. It seems silly, but I felt better.

Henry was a recognized, successful architect. I was a well-known champion and celebrity in the bridge world. We supported each other completely and our marriage allowed us to thrive individually.

So when he developed Alzheimer's disease in his last few years, I gave him the same love and support I'd always provided. I'd had confidence that as a capable nurse, I would be able to keep Henry whole. But I watched helplessly as he deteriorated. Some days he was lucid—even at the end—but most days he was utterly lost. My best friends during that time were hope and denial, and most days they visited in tandem. Henry succumbed to his illness in 2018. I was devastated. I had loved him dearly.

At 91, I have outlived three husbands. I am alone once more. My blessings abound, however; I live surrounded by the warmth, love, and support of my family and friends. I am grateful I can still enjoy my children and grandchildren, and have a positive outlook on life, although I can't say I like being old. My voyage continues—and they are my crew.

Reflections of a Chinese-American

Truth to Power

They say that 'speaking truth to power' means to stand up for what's right, to tell people in charge what's what. I've done a lot of that in my ten decades. I must say I feel great pride, not only for my actions, but also that I am able to remember them so clearly.

In high school we studied the writings of Abraham Lincoln and other civil libertarians; their philosophies got me thinking about the nature of the social system of my own country, where the lower classes were given little consideration. When I returned home during vacation, I would criticize my parents for their tacit acceptance of the coolie class, and I refused to travel by rickshaw in protest.

Another time I spoke out was when we were living in Shanghai. My father had been imprisoned for alleged communist ties. I managed to convince his university colleagues to accompany me to the prison and argue for his release. I look back and marvel that I had the courage to do that!

My age never kept me from recognizing wrongs that I could right. One of the achievements that gave me the most satisfaction was when I was in my teens. My mother had fallen severely ill. This was during our "mud hut" days in Chungking, and the inhospitable environment had taken its toll on Mother. She was bedridden and in horrible pain.

Father had written numerous letters to the American health authorities in Chungking requesting a doctor's assistance, to no avail. Ultimately, Father convinced a local doctor to come.

We were all appalled by Dr. Ting, whose disheveled appearance was matched by his rushed, perfunctory examination. "Tuberculosis," he pronounced tersely. He suggested no medication, no steps towards a cure; his only advice was that we should protect ourselves with masks and boil anything she'd touched. He suggested a special diet to regain her strength.

I couldn't accept Dr. Ting's dismissal of my mother. It was clear to me that Mother was not getting the medical treatment that she desperately needed. Her cough was violent and she was experiencing delusional episodes. Without asking my father's permission, I wrote a letter to Miss Peterson, my high school nurse, for advice.

Her letter arrived the following day. She indicated that Mother's symptoms didn't fit Dr. Ting's diagnosis, and suggested we contact Dr. Li, a local chest disease specialist, for another opinion. Father was furious with me that I'd written to Miss Peterson and refused to contact Dr. Li, arguing that doing so would make Dr. Ting lose face.

Dr. Li was a well-known physician who had lost both legs in a train accident. He lived in seclusion and refused almost all patients. Without telling my father, I took off to find Dr. Li and try to convince him to make a house call. The logistics of my mission were no impediment to my determination.

I traveled to the outskirts of Chungking and took a ferry to Mount Pehpei, the aptly named "Village of the Dying." I walked up an unpaved dirt road lined with ramshackle huts and homeless beggars. Emaciated children with bloated stomachs squatted on the ground, drinking brackish rainwater and chewing pieces of tree bark. The smell of human waste and illness left me gagging. Cat-sized rats roamed the area at their leisure.

When I finally arrived at the clinic, I was dismayed to find that Dr. Li lived on a mountaintop not even close to the clinic! The doctor in charge scoffed at me when I asked for a letter of introduction. I'd hoped I could convince him to come back with me to treat Mother. "Even if you could succeed in convincing Dr. Li to help you, where is your American jeep to drive you to the crest of the mountain—and then transport both of you back to your neighborhood?" Desperation made me brazen. I asked him if he might provide me with transportation that I needed, and amazingly, he granted my request. A few hours later, a jeep with an American serviceman came to pick me up.

We found Dr. Li in his home, bundled in his wheelchair, his lower torso covered by a blanket. How could this old man be the famous doctor? My disbelief gave me the courage to ask him to accompany me and treat my mother. He laughed at my request.

"Dr. Li does not practice medicine anymore," he replied, shaking his ancient head.

"Please doctor, you must come," I implored. "There is nothing I *must* do," he responded. "Go, you disrespectful girl, and leave me in peace!"

I left, but waited outside. Two hours passed. Finally I reentered the house and fell to my knees, kowtowing. I pleaded with him again on behalf of my mother, invoking his sense of duty to patients, humbling myself before him. I must have worn him down, because he blurted out, "Ok, ok, I'll go. If I don't go, will you ever leave my hallway?" He added, "Don't think you've forced me to do this, little girl. I've agreed for another reason." (What that reason was, I never discovered.) The steadfast American jeep driver brought us to my house in one and a half hours. Dr. Li examined Mother and pronounced that she did not have tuberculosis, but pleurisy—an inflammation of the lungs that causes sharp pains that worsen during breathing. But there was medicine that could cure it! Dr. Li was wonderful.

"See?" Mother wheezed, upon hearing the diagnosis. "That quack Dr. Ting would have killed me."

I went to bed that night fearful that father would surely come into my room and scold me for going to find Dr. Li without his permission. But that never happened. From my perspective, however, I felt that it was my father's responsibility to care for his wife. It shouldn't have fallen on the shoulders of a 14-year-old to save her mother's life. For the first time, I realized that my beloved, 'perfect' father had his imperfections—and that realization saddened me.

Over the next few months, I helped nurse Mother back to health.

I expected things to be different in the country of Abraham Lincoln, but when I was a nursing administrator, an incident forced me once again to use my voice. Two of my nurses were having an animated conversation. One was white, the other, Black. At one point in the conversation, the Black nurse touched her colleague's arm to make a point. The white nurse recoiled. "Take your cotton-pickin' hands off me!" Her choice of words outraged me. I wasn't familiar with the expression, but I had seen *Gone with the Wind,* and I knew those words were hurtful. "We are all nurses here," I admonished. "No one is better than anyone else."

Saving Galinda's father brought me great pleasure.

Galinda Wang was Charles' niece. When Charles and I lived in New York, Galinda lived in the same building, and we became good friends. She was like a daughter to me. Galinda had emigrated from Taiwan when she was eighteen, and after graduating from the Fashion Institute of Technology, she became an overnight fixture in the industry. She started her own house, *La Chine Classics,* with only $5,000 and built it into a $20 million enterprise. *La Chine* became one of the leading manufacturers of fashionable clothing for working women in the U.S. At one time, *La Chine* and the sister label, *Galinda,* could be seen in over 3000 stores in the U.S. Her collections ranged from beautiful sheer blouses to luxurious quilted velvet jacket and pants outfits.

Kathie is wearing one of Galinda's creations. She was a model for Galinda's company—in her spare time!

Galinda's father lived in Taiwan where he held the prominent role of Chiang Kai-shek's chief of staff. Accused of receiving bribes, he was summarily sent to jail. When I came to know Galinda, he had been languishing in prison for fifteen years.

I had a recognizable name; political leaders in Taiwan and in mainland China knew me for coaching their bridge teams to success in international competition. In addition, Charles and I had our shipping business and we negotiated trade deals with the political and commercial leaders in mainland China. I knew the right people in high places, both in Asia and in the U.S. I wanted to help Galinda's father.

We called the Chinese Consulate (Taiwan at that time) in New York and made an appointment to meet with one of the officials there. Upon our arrival, we were greeted by a cordial Consulate General. I stated the purpose for our visit, stressing the advanced age of Galinda's father, nearly 80, and reminding him that her father had been sent to jail without a trial. "Perhaps," I suggested in my most diplomatic tone, "reopening this case might be the proper thing to do." I made it clear that my political clout with many U.S. Congress people, plus an immediate visit to top media outlets, including *CNN* and *The New York Times,* might cast the Taiwanese government in an undesirable light.

Taiwan was sensitive about maintaining a good reputation in the eyes of the international community. Five days after meeting with the Consulate General, he notified me that Galinda's father was released from prison and sent home.

Take Me Out to the Ballgame

Being American has offered me great advantage, even privilege. It is no wonder, then, that I was eager to embrace American culture wholeheartedly.

When I first arrived in the U.S., I heard that

baseball was America's national pastime, and that it was "as American as apple pie." The cultural historian, Jacques Barzun says, "Whoever wants to know the heart and mind of America had better learn baseball, the rules, and reality of the game."

I really wanted to be an authentic "Yankee Doodle Dandy"—so I needed to learn about baseball. I lived in New York City, so I *had* to follow the Yankees! Roger Maris, Mickey Mantle, and Phil Rizzuto became household names. Holy cow! I even attended a Yankees game once and had a great seat near the dugout. Tickets cost more than I could afford, so I didn't go often.

But really, I needed baseball. Baseball idioms were part of American culture and the English language. It wasn't enough to be fluent; I had to sound like an American, and that meant knowing the jargon.

In no time at all, I was slinging the slang like a true New Yorker:

"Of course his fees are high. He's a big league lawyer."

"I'm doing more than I need to do, just to make sure my bases are covered."

"I can't believe you said that. You really threw me a curveball."

"Did you get to first base on your date?"

"Wow, your idea at the meeting really hit it out of the ballpark."

"That idea really came from left field."

"They never anticipated the sudden drop in

prices. Now it's a whole new ballgame."

I knew I'd hit a home run when I was able to enjoy the wit and wisdom of Yogi Berra.

"Nobody goes there anymore; it's too crowded!"

"We made too many wrong mistakes."

"You can observe a lot by just watching."

...and my favorite, "It ain't over til it's over."

"I'm in Heaven"

One year Charles asked me what I wanted for my birthday. With no hesitation I replied, "I want to dance with Fred Astaire or to play bridge with the great international champion Benito Garozzo." Surprisingly—or not—Astaire wasn't available, so my birthday present was Garozzo, a successful and brilliant member of the Italian bridge team. I got to play with him, and he taught me so much more about the game.

But I *really* wanted to dance with Fred Astaire.

I fell in love with dancing in high school in Chungking, at the Academy of Performing Arts. Mother was enamored with Western culture, so she allowed me this pleasure. Dai Ailian was my dancing instructor. A former student of Martha Graham, Ms. Dai went on to help China build a generation of dancers and choreographers, and became known in China as the "Mother of Chinese Modern Dance." I acted as the Chinese/English interpreter between her and the students, since Chinese wasn't her native language and she spoke it haltingly.

When Kathie returned to China after three decades, Ms. Dai, her former dance teacher was high on her list of people she had to see.

Through that role, I got to know my fellow students and Ms. Dai much better.

I loved and appreciated the new world that Ms. Dai opened for me. Dancing is often seen as interpreting music with your body, or describing life with your movement. When I danced, I felt free and alive. While we studied both ballet and modern dance, I found a home in the modern style. Classical ballet seemed to have a bunch of rules that one was obligated to follow. Dancing provided for me an escape from the ravages of war-torn China, and Ms. Dai mentored my entrance into this graceful world.

When, six months later, it became obvious that I was taking dance much more seriously than Mother had intended, she pulled me out of that school and sent me back to the Baptist missionary school, claiming that it was dishonorable for a woman of our social status to perform in public. Mother's decision only temporarily short-circuited my interest in dance.

I had to wait until I was attending college to have my next dance lessons. My first American male friend was the son of my father's friend. Joe Field was a captain in the U.S. Army who was stationed in Shanghai. When Joe wasn't in service, he lived in Miami, Florida and taught ballroom dancing at the Arthur Murray Studio. Joe was full of vitality; he was a born dancer. What he lacked in looks he made up for in grace and humor—he was so much fun! More importantly, he was willing to teach me to dance.

To my great surprise, Mother was thrilled that I had an American friend. Joe introduced me to the glamour of ballroom dancing. I'd never realized that each dance could transport me to such different places. When we waltzed, I could be gliding through old-world Vienna. The jitterbug gave me the chance to cut loose and show my mischievous side. (I'd often think back to my jerky antics as a child, imitating the flappers of the '20s for Mother's guests.) Ballroom rhumba was slower and more controlled than the frenzied Cuban dance, but I still got to sway my hips! We were frequently invited to dancing parties to exhibit.

However, my favorite dance was the tango, so precise and dramatic. When I was dancing the tango with Joe, I would feel like a passionate Argentinian *bailarin* as we swooped and dipped together.

We practiced whenever we could at home, under the watchful eyes of Mother. Joe and I became one of the best dancing teams in Shanghai. Before long, we were invited to many dancing parties to exhibit our new and innovative dance routines. The dancing parties led to professional competitions, and we won many trophies and titles. The applause was exhilarating. I thought of Fred Astaire's song, "Cheek to Cheek" and I completely agreed: I was in heaven!

I never forgot Ms. Dai, though I lost touch with her for decades. In 1980 I returned to China for the first time after emigrating to the U.S. I asked the handler that the Chinese authorities assigned to me if he would locate Ms. Dai for me. She was living in an area reserved for Overseas Chinese who had returned to China. I knocked at the door of her apartment, fearful that she might not remember me, but upon opening her door her eyes lit with recognition. "Ah yes," she said slowly, "I remember you. You were that student who loved dance but wanted shortcuts to learning."

I entered her studio and was enveloped by the smell of varnished wood floors. Brass barres lined the mirrored walls, and as I looked at my middle-aged reflection, I was transported back to that period under her tutelage. Her sparkling and influential personality had made my dancing months an important part of my development.

Four decades later, I asked a friend to do an Internet search for Ms. Dai. She found a brief biographical sketch on Wikipedia. I'm so happy that her accomplishments have found their way into the 21st century!

Confluences/Influences

I like to think of my life as a flowing together of people, incidents, and good fortune. While several events of my childhood in China still haunt me, they are tempered by the grace and good will of my many guides and teachers. Our family cook, Lao Chang, opened my eyes to hidden treasures of China. He was also my best friend.

Our family was constantly on the run from the Japanese invasion and bombings. Living in different places didn't afford me the opportunity to make long-term friendships with kids my own age. Lao Chang was a kind, intelligent man who took the time to talk with me, served as a confidant, and taught me skills to negotiate life.

Lao is a special word that literally means "old" but it's also used as sign of cordial respect, rather than an indication of someone's age. It sometimes has a special connotation, as in the English expression, "Hi there, old friend," where "old" can signify both respect and endearment.

When we were teenagers living in Shanghai, he took Alice and me on our first picnic in Peking. He showed us how to make Chinese lamb sandwiches, and we feasted on them as we lounged on the deck

Lao Chang opened our eyes and ears to the Peking Opera.

of the marble boat in the former Empress's summer palace.

Lao Chang introduced us to the Forbidden City; he led us through museum halls, searching for access to the maze of dilapidated courtyards and winding alleys, now closed to the public, where the Imperial family and their servants once walked.

When he traveled outdoors, Lao Chang would carry a folded newspaper under his arm so people would think that he was an educated man. While he did not have a formal education, he was extremely knowledgeable on numerous topics. He was rich in his own philosophies and ideas but he also taught us our basic Chinese history. He often read us Chinese literature, religious articles, and Confucian philosophy.

He would act and sing the roles from his favorite operas, to give us a flavor of each story. I clung to his every word, note, and gesture. By the time I finally attended a real opera in Peking, I was already familiar with the libretti and plots, thanks to our talented family cook.

He was a proud, but also confused, man. He was both for and against the dynastic and republican forms of government, pro-and anti-Buddhism. He claimed to support Mao Zedong, yet he worshipped the founder of the Chinese republic, Sun Yat-sen. He had unsophisticated revolutionary ideas about personal freedom and republicanism. He hated the dictatorship and repression that the Chinese endured under Chiang Kai-shek, yet he didn't want to leave our family to join the revolution.

I asked my sister once, "Don't you just love Lao Chang?"

Alice looked at me, thinly veiling her disdain. "He is good enough at what he was hired to do. He is our cook. You don't love a cook." This was how I was introduced to class differences.

Our cook's life ended suddenly and tragically. It was the summer of 1947, the turbulent times of the civil war with the Chinese communists. Lao Chang was arrested, blindfolded and displayed in the main square in the center of Shanghai. There, with no trial, he was shot by Chiang Kai-shek's soldiers. After hearing the news, I tried to retrieve his body so we could bury him properly.

The authorities informed me that the bodies of traitors had been dumped into a mass grave at the south side of Shanghai.

For days, I locked myself in my room crying and thinking about revenge. What could I do to pay them back for murdering a man who had never hurt anyone in his life? I even thought about going out at night to set fire to the government's political party headquarters. I wanted to start a riot in protest.

Eventually my father helped me through my anger and confusion. "This is a bad time for free thinking people in China," Father said. "I am sure that Lao Chang would not want you to get into trouble with the law or Chiang's government by avenging his treatment. The best way for you to re-member him is to keep on believing and fighting for justice and freedom for China."

He then counseled me to go through Lao Chang's personal belongings—he feared the govern-ment would look for evidence of his "crimes."

Under Lao Chang's bed, I found a diary and a bundle of essays that he had written. There were books by Mao Zedong, Sun Yat-sen, Confucius and many contemporary writers like Lu Xun, whose works served, for many intellectuals, as a cry of protest against our country's social injustice and oppression. Lao Chang also had works by Lao She, whose novel *Rickshaw Boy* would become a U.S. "Book of the Month Club" selection in 1945. Both authors' books were later burned by the Red Guard, casualties of the Cultural Revolution. I hid all this evidence under my bed and took it out to read whenever I missed my best friend.

Lao Chang's thoughts, his kindness, and compassion continued to influence me. His essays and books shaped many of my life's beliefs, my faith in the goodness of humanity, and my political views all through my life.

Not all those who have influenced me were my contemporaries. Qu Yuan lived from 340–278 BCE. He was a poet and politician, a patriot who spoke truth to power. His outspoken voice led to his exile, during which time he composed some of the greatest poetry in Chinese literature. His poems lamented the corruption of the government and his desire to remain pure nevertheless. In 278 BCE, he committed suicide by drowning; many attribute his death to the loss of faith in his beloved but failing motherland. Others see his death as a type of martyrdom: the ultimate way to protect his life principles. Qu Yuan's poetry was banned during the Cultural Revolution because Mao Zedong feared the poet's ideas and the influence he might have on the populace.

We honor and pay tribute to Qu Yuan during my favorite holiday, *Qingming Jie,* known in English as "Tomb Sweeping Day." (Many of my friends are surprised that the Chinese New Year is not, in fact, my holiday of choice. If you had grown up as I did, surrounded by the explosions of wartime bombs, you might understand how the sudden *bangs* and *pops* of fireworks leave me nervous and shaking.) On this day, families visit the tombs of their departed relatives and ancestors to clean their gravesites, make ritual offerings, and offer prayers of remembrance and respect. Qu Yuan's story is one of sacrifice for fundamental ideals of freedom, and his last poem, written shortly before his death, is recited yearly by intellectuals and peasants alike. It has become a symbol of the Chinese peoples' will to oppose tyranny, and in it, I hear echoes of Patrick Henry's "Give me liberty or give me death."

> Endlessly the road goes on
> How long! How long!
> Ever seeking in high places and low
> I plod on
> For what my heart loves
> I would die
> Nine times over
> With no regret.
> —the poetry of Qu Yuan (340-278 BCE)

I remember my grandfather and father commemorating Qu Yuan and celebrating the Qingming festival when I was growing up in China. During the holiday, Chinese celebrants traditionally eat *zong-zi,* a sticky rice dumpling, to commemorate the villagers who, unsuccessful in saving their beloved poet from drowning, threw rice into the water as a food offering to him in the afterlife, as well as to keep the fish away from ravaging his body. The boat race to search for his body ultimately became the cultural tradition of dragon boat racing, held on the anniversary of his death.

Chinese or American?

There is a Chinese expression that translates literally as "not Chinese and not Western" (*bu-Zhung, bu-xi* in Pinyin, or *bu-Chong, bu-hsi*) : "neither fish nor fowl." That would describe me. I'm—both and neither—not Chinese and not Western. At the age of 91, I'm still searching for myself!

There is an American saying, "You can take the boy out of Brooklyn, but you can't take Brooklyn out of the boy." Change "Brooklyn" to "China" and you have my story. I was born and raised in China, so the culture is, and always will be, part of me.

At the same time, having lived in the U.S. for more than 70 years, I am also very much American, and my thoughts and habits are probably more American than Chinese at this point in my life. I'm a naturalized American citizen, and my heart still swells with pride whenever I hear the *Star Spangled Banner.* Though English is not my native language, I have been speaking it for almost as long as I've spoken Chinese, and both my written and spoken English are better than my native language. Writing in Chinese requires a lot of memorization, and it's easy to forget. My spoken Mandarin Chinese is also rusty—language, like muscles, weakens if you don't use it. Even though I see myself as 100% American, however, there are those to whom I will always be seen as 100% Asian—or Chinese to those who know me—regardless of how many years I have lived in the U.S.

Many years ago, our family had the opportunity to visit Hong Kong, a benefit of Chang-Jui's employment at the United Nations. We had not been allowed at the time to visit mainland China, so the U.N. sent us to Hong Kong as part of our home leave, where we could stay connected to our culture. Ada was overwhelmed: she had never seen so many people who looked like her, who used pedicabs and spoke a Chinese dialect that she did not recognize.

In 2012 Ada reflected on her Hong Kong experience:

> Abroad, we were treated like visiting
> royalty. Back home we were ordinary
> people living ordinary lives in the some-
> times harsh and mean streets of New
> York City. Abroad we were exoticized
> for our American-ness. Back home we
> were stereotyped because of our Asian
> faces and culture. This was all very con-
> fusing. My father worked hard to teach
> us that wealth, perceived wealth and
> privilege were fleeting and not based on
> merit or character, and that they were
> corruptive and not worthy of pursuing. I
> remember him taking me to the famous
> Peninsula Hotel in Hong Kong, a place
> of ultimate colonialist white privilege,
> and pointing to the uniformed door-
> man and guests, and then walking me

around to the back and pointing to the place where a sign by a water fountain saying "Dogs and Chinamen" had hung during his childhood. And his anger at being mistaken for a Japanese in the streets of Tokyo."[9]

So many years have passed, and I still have respect and admiration for both cultures. However, as I enter my 10th decade, the specter of COVID an international menace, I find that my comfortable place in the United States can no longer be taken for granted. Being Chinese-American has become a liability. Some people in this country, influenced by the media, have referred to this pandemic as "the Chinese virus"—and the consequences have taken their toll on all Asians. I have read stories of individuals here, in my country, avoiding Asian-looking people on the street, or worse, verbally or physically threatening them. We are accused of spreading the virus throughout the world, causing a global plague. I have heard the expression "breathing while Asian": moments when people of Asian descent are afraid of being spat at, or assaulted. Chinese restaurants have been forced to close. Many Asian-Americans who have lived in this country their whole lives have been told "Go back to China, where you belong." I thought I was finished with running.

Nevertheless, I am extremely grateful to have both ways of life as part of my cultural-DNA make-up. I am fortunate to have had my three children born into a kinder, less divisive America, and hope and pray the same can be said of their children's children, especially in these troubled times. But here lingers my life-long problem, trying to decide how best to clearly define myself. In China, I was the "second daughter" scorned by my mother and constantly striving for love and acceptance. In the U.S., my arranged marriage left me in the shadow of my husband, figuratively walking three paces behind him. I was a wife, young mother, housekeeper, and cook. It was only later, when I began a life outside the home—as a nurse, then nursing administrator, bridge player, and business consultant—that I saw who I could be.

A favorite poem expresses my early feelings of being randomly blown and tossed around throughout my life:

The Winds of Fate

One ship drives east and another
drives west
With the self-same winds that blow;

'Tis the set of the sails
And not the gales
That tells them the way to go.

Like the winds of the sea are the
winds of fate
As we voyage along through life;
'Tis the set of the soul
That decides its goal

And not the calm or the strife.

—Ella Wheeler Wilcox

Fortunately, I learned how to take the rudder.

Mother

In *Second Daughter* I first wrote of my conflicted feelings toward my mother, hoping to help other young women who might have similar issues. People associated with the release of that book almost refused to publish it. "Nice girls do not talk about their mothers, especially when they are Chinese," I was told. Fortunately, some last minute editing saved the book. I find it ironic that forty years later, "tell all" books reveal the private details of families' lives. I certainly don't relish speaking ill of my mother—or anyone—so the challenge will be for me to provide a balanced and objective description of our relationship.

Born in Shanghai to a merchant family, Mother was a fiercely intelligent and forceful woman. She had an uncompromisingly strong will, and knew how to control people for her own advantage. She had an innate understanding of interpersonal dynamics and was skilled at using crude psychological tactics to achieve her own wants. No one disobeyed her.

Despite her tiny four-foot ten-inch frame, she had a way of making her presence known and felt whenever she entered a room. She wore her glittering jewels and fashionable clothing like an empress.

She was power incarnate—her presence generated fear, but also anticipation of something wonderful.

Mother's light complexion was a sign of social status in China, and she saw herself as socially superior. She didn't work, wasn't darkened by the sun's rays, much as ancient Chinese royalty let their nails grow to absurd lengths to show they led a life of indolence. However, Mother was anything but idle. She was extremely capable and ambitious; she just did not have a career outside the home. She certainly could have excelled in any profession of her choosing, and in a more modern era, she would have been the most liberated of women.

My maternal grandmother had her feet bound, as was the tradition, but she didn't make her daughter submit to that horrible and painful ordeal, despite the fact that in the first decade of the 1900s, the custom was fairly commonplace. Neither my sisters nor I were forced to have our feet bound either. Moreover, in an era where arranged marriages were the norm, Mother persuaded her brother-in-law to introduce her to her future husband—my father— and married him one year later.

At all times a non-conformist, my mother begged for and received a modern education at a Christian school in Shanghai. She decided to become Christian, not from religious conviction, but because the Protestant missionaries of that time opposed foot-binding, concubines, and supported equality of the sexes: all ideals that she valued. (She chose Protestantism over Catholicism, not out of any particular disagreement with religious dogma, but because she didn't relish meatless Fridays!)

Mother directed Father's career for him, assisting in his rise to prominence. She decided where he would teach, when he should publish, what promotions he should seek, accept, or decline, and which political and academic contacts he should cultivate. Despite his intellectual brilliance, she recognized in him a social naïveté that required her guidance and direction.

My three sisters and I were given both Chinese and English names, and my mother spent a fortune on our education and upbringing. She lived through her daughters, yet always demanded personal recognition for herself.

My birth and presence in her life was a constant reminder of Mother's failure to produce a male heir. When my older sister Alice was born, there was some disappointment that she wasn't a boy, but there was still hope for the second child. For my entire teenage and adult life, Mother blamed me for not being a boy. Her judgment reflected that of her society, and I lived with this shame and accepted it as my due.

For thousands of years, Chinese families practiced female infanticide by tossing unwanted girls down wells. As a young girl, I was told that I should be grateful for having been spared this horrible fate; what were hurtful words in comparison? This veiled threat kept me from complaining about my lot in life for many years, but the psychological damage left me feeling numb and unwanted. Sometimes I marvel at my ability to speak up for myself during my adolescence—was it because of or despite her cruelty? Many years later, on the publication of my first autobiography, I pledged my share of the royalties to the prevention of child abuse. I have known this torment.

In 1980, I visited my mother for the first time in thirty-two years. My father was ailing and I wanted to give my mother another chance. Maybe I had been immature? Maybe I'd failed to appreciate her? My sisters, however, had already colored my perception. Over the years, they'd written me letters including stories that began with, "Do you know what she did? Again?" We really had no chance at reconciliation.

As my father lay dying in his hospital bed, mother released her accusations, pent-up for so many years. "How dare you divorce the husband I picked for you?" Chang-Jui was her choice, so our divorce caused her to lose face. The irony of her words was not lost on me, nor was her unwillingness to acknowledge that I had finally found happiness and love with my second husband. She spared no vitriol. She was disappointed in my nursing career and did not approve of the adult I had become.

I remember the 1983 movie, *Terms of Endearment,* with Shirley MacLaine and Debra Winger. As I had sat in the dark theater, I was jealous of that mother-daughter relationship, the unconditional love, the laughing and sharing. Maybe my mother resented my strength; maybe she was intimidated by my own competitive spirit. I thought of my own children and hoped that I had been a better mother. Despite my gifts, assistance, and good intentions, nothing had changed between my mother and me. I had to face the fact that I could not love my mother, nor did I even like her. Being with her was destructive. I had to move on.

Many years later, Henry Sender and I attended services at our synagogue during the Yom Kippur holiday. We recited a blessing for departed family and friends. I prayed for my mother.

> My dear mother, may she rest in peace.
> I am grateful for her gift of life, and for
> the goodness and kindness with which
> she touched my life that helped me to
> share those qualities with others. With
> contrite heart, I repent of my thoughts
> or acts, which may be pardoned by you.

Reciting this prayer gave peace to my aching heart. I was grateful for the solace.

My life has been full, replete with love, success, and acceptance. I have found it, maybe not where I was searching, but where it has found me.

My family and friends in the U.S. have embraced me, given me strength, and I have wholeheartedly accepted their warmth, love, and encouragement.

I'm all right, Mother.

The Bridge Magicians

The Game of Bridge: Why is it Special?

"Bridge is the most entertaining and
intelligent card game the wit of man has
so far devised."

—Warren Buffet

Bridge challenges you both emotionally and
intellectually. It contains elements of planning
and organization, and requires that first and foremost you communicate with your partner effectively. Attempting to use ineffective bridge language is
like trying to carve a diamond with a pickaxe. You
must be a detective, trying to infer which unseen
cards are held by your partner and the opponents.
A successful play at bridge can make one swoon
with happiness. Certain rare bridge players—those
brilliant and creative experts—are able to turn mere
cards of paper into totems imbued with personality and power. They make miracles happen at the
bridge table. I call them "the bridge magicians."

Bridge has been my love and joy throughout my
adult life. I am fortunate to have met many wonderful, talented, interesting, and warm people through
the game. Some of those people are the bridge partners with whom I have won major bridge tournaments. While my trophy case at home is filled with
many awards and trophies (including 4 gold and 4
silver medals for international competition), they

pale in comparison to the real gems of my life—my three cherished children, my grandchildren and great-grandchildren. I have shared my life with three husbands, all amazing, talented, and gifted in their own right.

Wan Li , Chairman of the Standing Committee of the National Peoples' Congress of China, received the Solomon Award from the International Bridge Press Association in 1985, for the "Best Played Hand of the Year." Deng Xiao Peng was jealous. He complained to me, "I got only the 'Best Personality of the Year award!' "

In addition to playing bridge, I have participated in bridge missions all over the world to promote the game. I have been the guest of such illustrious partners as the former Premier of the People's Republic of China, Deng Xiaoping, and Golda Meir of Israel. Major celebrities, Oprah Winfrey,

Sammy Davis, Jr., and Omar Sharif among them, have appeared at charitable events that I have hosted. In 1986, the International Bridge Press Association (IBPA) named me the Bridge Personality of the Year, an award bestowed on my friend Deng Xiaoping five years earlier.

Sammy Davis Jr. was the guest of honor at a fundraiser Kathie organized through the American Contract Bridge League.

I have been working on this book, a labor of love, for many years. At the age of 91, I recognize that this is likely my last written contribution to the world of bridge. I invite you to meet some of the bridge notables with whom I share a history. Hopefully you will come to feel, as I do, that the game is more than just about winning.

Daniel Hollingshead, a contributor to the *American Contract League Bridge Bulletin*, writes: "Bridge requires the complex visualization of chess and 'go,' the social composure and mind-reading powers of poker and a level of cooperation with your partner unlike any game that I know of."[10]

Not only is bridge enjoyed as a social pastime, it is also great exercise for the brain. In fact, recent studies have suggested that mentally challenging activities like bridge can help delay the onset of dementia. And 'Bridge' lives up to its name: it joins together people from all over the world. Bridge players never need to feel lonely; wherever you go, you can pretty much be guaranteed that right around the corner is a table with a North, South, and East, needing a West!

C.C. Wei Develops Precision

Charles—known to the bridge world as C.C.—started to play bridge as a hobby, but as an entrepreneur, he was fascinated with the successes of the international bridge teams. He knew that the Italian Blue Team had had a string of wins for a number of decades and was challenged to discover why this was so. One day, uninvited, Charles entered the office of Edgar Kaplan, editor of *The Bridge World Magazine*, and foremost authority in the field. "Why does the Italian team always win?" he demanded.

"Because they have a better bidding system" was the response.

Kaplan's answer, while succinct, wasn't entirely accurate. There were a number of reasons why the Italians had been formidable competitors for years: their brilliance and imagination were matched by their cohesion as a team and complete dedication to the game.

At the end of the 1960s, two major businessmen created teams to compete against the Blue Team. One was Ira Corn, who gathered six talented young players to form the Aces; the other was C.C. Wei. Charles was determined to create a new bidding system based on mathematics and logic to challenge the Blue Team's Big Club system. Richard Frey, one of the best American players, wrote that Wei devoted "endless hours to a search for a theoretical method based on one of his own major specialties, mathematics. The result was the Precision Club System."[11] True to its name, playing Precision gives you a precise image of the hand early in the bidding before opponents can get in their own bids.

Charles faced challenges from the onset. Despite his confidence in Precision, bridge experts were reluctant to try it out in competition. They were too frequently approached by people touting the 'next great thing' in bidding systems. However, his unassuming personality and dogged persistence paid off. He approached bridge notables Richard Frey, Alan Truscott, and Tom Smith with his ideas, and together they fine-tuned the Precision system.

As the system matured, Charles engaged the Chinese Taipei team, whom he had begun coaching, to enter the Far Eastern zonal bridge competition in 1968. Charles, a decent player, didn't enjoy the cut-throat attitude of tournament bridge. Nevertheless, he was an outstanding coach, and under his direction, the Taipei team qualified to compete in the prestigious Bermuda Bowl held the following year. They were the first team to use the Precision system.

One afternoon in 1968, Charles came home, thrumming with excitement. "Kathie! We have been asked to manage the Taipei team! We are going to Rio!"

The World Bridge Federation had asked Charles to sponsor the team at the 1969 Bermuda Bowl in Brazil. He was invited to be a non-playing captain, not because of his experience, but because the team needed a financial sponsor. I was totally nonplussed. "But I'm only a novice bridge player myself! I've never managed a team before. Besides—I have my own job!"

"But Kathie, you can do it. I have complete confidence in you."

He handed me a large box of books, including the classics *Morehead on Bidding* and Watson's *The Play of the Hand*, and added with a grin, "besides, no one will expect our team to even survive the first cut. Trust me, you will enjoy the experience."

So I agreed, subject to two conditions: one, I would have sole power to choose the team from among the Chinese bridge players, and two, the players would have to follow my strict rules.

Immediately I had to research and familiarize

myself with the competition: who bid aggressively or conservatively, bridge methods, even which team members had annoying or rude personalities. I also learned the bidding systems that our team would likely encounter. The Italians used variations of the Blue Club, others used systems similar to 2/1, and at least one team played 4-card majors, instead of a standard 5-card major opening. Lastly, I had to teach them English. Bridge was played in English internationally, and many of the Taipei Team members didn't know simple terms like 'double' or 'redouble' in the language in which they would compete. The prospect was daunting.

To complicate matters more, it became clear that our team was not accustomed to local Brazilian cuisine, so I had to add "chef" to my growing list of responsibilities. I had to import ingredients from neighboring Sao Paolo, a city with a large Chinese population, since Rio was sorely lacking. Finding someone who could translate for me was another problem: I spoke no Portuguese, and didn't know how to explain words like "garlic" and "ginger." Finally a young bilingual man offered to help me out, and I promised him a meal in return. Fifteen people had been invited to my first Chinese meal, but when word got around, over thirty showed up! So our team was well fed, and I also made sure that they kept regular hours. As a nurse, I was attentive to their health.

I wanted to make sure that our team would really stand out in a crowd. Typically, men's tournaments were formal affairs, so we rented elegant tuxedos for our players. We entered the hall and were surprised to see that no one was dressed up. I did get my wish though—we were certainly noticed!

The Taipei team was the big underdog. Few people were interested in watching them play. However, when expatriate Chinese from Sao Paulo heard that an Asian team was playing, many stopped by to kibitz and root us on. To almost everyone's surprise, the team came through and won a Silver medal, beating the U.S. team and losing only to the Italians. Alan Truscott summed up the team's advantage in his recap in *The New York Times*: "... they were able to perform with such success [due] to the simplicity and effectiveness of Wei's "Precision" system ..."[12]

Our team had the disadvantage of limited experience in international competition and little experience playing together as a team, while the Italian team had amassed over 24 international titles. I would like to think that my sound administrative ability and experience in dealing with people in high-pressure situations helped me, as a coach and manager, to lessen some of our challenges.

Our win gave Precision instant recognition: bridge players of all levels now wanted to use it. At least five books on the Precision System were published the following year, and even some of the Italian teams switched!

After placing second in the 1969 World Championships, Precision had other successes in the '70s:

- Taiwan, 1970 World Championships, 2nd place
- U.S. Summer National Team Championships 1970 and 1971
- Vanderbilt Spring National Knockout Team Championship 1972
- Precision teams won both the Men's and the Women's Team-of-Four Championships at the 1971 U.S. Spring National Tournament.

Bridge is constantly evolving as a game, and as a result, new bidding systems have become popular over the years. However, Precision is still used at international bridge competitions, and of course, by me!

Kathie interviews Warren Buffet for CCTV and Sinovision before Corporate vs Congress Bridge Match.

An Interview with Warren Buffet

"The magic word is bridge. May I speak with Mr. Buffet?" With these words I managed to secure an interview with one of the world's richest men.

Warren Buffet had been interviewed by writers from many publications, but never from a bridge player turned writer. I introduced myself and the magazine, The American Contract Bridge League's monthly periodical, proudly citing our over a quarter million readership. His response was both immediate and gracious, and within a few days, I flew to Omaha, armed with a tape recorder, camera, and a few bridge hands.

The appearance of the Berkshire Hathaway building at Kiewit Plaza belies the enormous wealth and power within: it is understated, even unprepossessing, with rows and rows of windows that looked like little teeth. Mr. Buffet himself was warm and friendly, a simple Midwesterner who just happened to have mastered the art of investing. His secretary provided me with refreshment—a Cherry Coke without ice—and we exchanged pleasantries. I told him my story of Sam Stayman, a famous bridge player and creator of one of the most frequently used bridge conventions.

"I used to tell bridge players that Sam Stayman was my partner. What I did not mention was that I was only his business partner—not his bridge partner. You would be surprised at how many really good bridge partners I was able to get as a result of that trick!" Buffet chuckled in appreciation. (Later I discovered that he'd been business partners with Sam Stayman as well.) After about an hour, with his permission, I switched on my tape recorder.

Kathie Wei: I have wanted to interview you ever since I read your profile in *Fortune* magazine. I like your sense of humor. You said that if you went to jail, you'd want your cellmates to be bridge players—so you must love the game. We've also read that you are a very good bridge player.

Warren Buffet: I'm not, really. I enjoy it enormously, but I don't play that well. I never played intensely for any period of my life. If I could take the amount of time I've played and condense it into a one-year period, I'd be a better player.

KW: Do you play bridge for excitement, entertainment, or relaxation?

WB: I get all three when playing bridge. I really do.

KW: What is it about bridge that turns you on?

WB: It's the most fascinating game around, and I have played a lot of games. It's even more fascinating than making money ... you should look at life like playing a bridge hand. You may pick up a string of Yarboroughs, [no-point hands] but you are going to get your share of the blockbusters, too. The trick is to play every hand as well as you can.

In our canning business, we make all kinds of money in December. We lose money in July. But we want to play in July just as well as we can and we want to play in December as well as we can. In the stock markets, for a couple of years, nothing pops up and then there are other times when it's raining gold; when it's raining gold you want to be out there with a ladle—you don't want a fork at that time. I feel the same way about bridge.

KW: Have you ever heard of Leonard Pennario? He's a famous concert pianist and he enjoys playing bridge. He has a problem, however. No matter how hard he tries to concentrate while playing bridge, music is always going through his mind. Can you banish everything from your mind when you sit down to play bridge?

WB: Everything else disappears from my mind. Sam Stayman used to be one of my business partners. [We] go back 27 years. Sam used to play with a businessman in New York who was a terrible bridge player. Sam said that every time this fellow would do something dumb at the bridge table, he would say a few seconds later, "I think I'll take that parking garage deal in Portland." And that was his excuse—that he was thinking about a buy. When I make a mistake it's because I make a mistake and not because I'm thinking about business.

KW: What got you started in bridge?

WB: College. I didn't play a lot, Kathie, and that was my problem. I went to the University of Pennsylvania and I played bridge there. But then I transferred to the University of Nebraska, where I lived off campus in a little apartment and didn't play a game of bridge for three or four years.

KW: Young people are not playing much bridge now.

WB: They're missing something.

KW: I have started a lot of scholarships to promote bridge. I feel that many players basically were taught bad bridge and I want to correct that. If young people play more bridge, they'll stay away from drugs and other destructive enticements.

WB: Two of my children now play bridge. The third is terribly interested in music, but he plays a little.

KW: Do you think bridge has a place in education?

WB: It's good mental exercise and it's a lot of fun. It develops the intellect.

KW: Do you play much duplicate [a type of tournament bridge]?

WB: I played duplicate bridge 15 years ago and then I did it four or five times afterwards. I enjoyed it, and if I were a traveling salesman or something like that, I absolutely would play duplicate as a way to spend time in strange towns. But rubber bridge [usually played at home] involves sitting down against people that I know really well—I enjoy that most.

KW: Do you feel a sense of gratification when you play a hand well?

WB: I feel gratification and I feel total disgust when I play one badly. I played last weekend … [for] about eight hours and I did something very dumb on the last hand and I am still thinking about it!

KW: Is it the same way when you are conducting business?

WB: I do more dumb things in bridge than I do in business, a lot more. You do some things that you are proud of, and you do some things that make you wonder how you could do something so stupidly. That's what keeps you coming back.

KW: Do you apply your knowledge of mathematics and business skill, or do you just play by the seat of your pants?

WB: Well, it's pretty much by the seat of my pants. I think in terms of probabilities by nature, so I am used to calculating a gain/loss ratio for many courses of action. I read a [bridge] book when I was in college by S. J. Simon *Why You Lose at Bridge,* and that fits my nature. The first couple of chapters are devoted to just figuring the odds. I can do that in an amateurish sort of way.

KW: Does your good business judgment help you in bridge?

WB: I think you do best when you think through probabilities in either business or bridge. You are essentially taking the cards as they are dealt and handling them the best way that you can. In bridge as well as in business, there are some very boring hands—some that don't pay to get busy and active about. But there are other times when you have to seize the opportunity.

There are lots of similarities between business and bridge. You have to face the world as it is, not as you want it to be. If you make the correct percentage plays day after day, week after week, year after year, it's going to work.

There's another similarity between bridge and business, of course; if you want mostly to win, the best way to do it is to play against weak opposition. This is even better than having a lot of skill, if all you are playing for is to win. The real test in business is weak opposition. Luck is not part of it. I never sit down at the bridge table and say I'm going to be lucky tonight. And I never sit down to a business deal that way, either.

KW: For an average bridge player—let's say just married, a new job, etc. What advice would you give him in business?

WB: That's a tough question. I would recommend some good books about investment. I couldn't give a simple answer on it. He would need to be like a good bridge player—you have to work very hard at it! You read a lot of bridge. You play a lot of bridge. Same with business. If you play bridge only once a month, you surely don't want to play with people who play all of the time. You would get in over your head. Same with business. To make some good investments, you have to invest a lot of time. You have to do your homework. Every year in business, I just make sure that I am ahead of where I was the previous year.

KW: Do you have any advice for young people about bridge, business and studying—such as why bridge might be a good basis for entering the business world?

WB: Good things will happen to them regardless. They have to enjoy what they do and beyond that everything is frosting on the cake. Anything that you have to think well to do well is going to have some form of transference. It's going to make your relations with other human beings better if you learn something about working with partnerships. The fellow I play with in New York, for example, is not a great player, but we get the best results possible because we work well with each other. That's the way that I work with the managers in my business—it's important to know how to deal with other human beings.

You can be the world's greatest bridge player, but someone else is going to be sitting across the table from you. If you behave in a way—any way—that inhibits that person from playing up to his or her potential, you are not going to get as good a result as you would if you knew how to work other human beings. It's terribly important.

KW: Bridge now gets all kinds of competition—computers, television, etc. Do you feel that we should update our management skills in promoting bridge?

WB: Sure. You might be able to do it by television, but the problem is that it takes a while to appreciate the game. You don't get a good enough grasp of the game in an hour to really appreciate it. It takes a certain amount of time, and that makes it tough to promote in an era of instant gratification. Anyone who spends the time to appreciate the subtleties of the game will be in for a lifetime of enjoyment.

KW: ...My late husband C.C. invented the Precision system [of bidding at bridge]. He sponsored many young people. He was interested in developing bridge and developing the system. He once sponsored a guy named Ronnie Rubin, who went off to play in a backgammon tournament and won $90,000. Ronnie bought himself a seat on the option trader's market and applied bridge theory to trading. Options has made him a fortune; in fact, many of the traders are good bridge players.

WB: It's tougher to be a top notch bridge player than it is to be a top notch businessman. I would think that any bridge player who applied the same intensity and time to his business would do well.

KW: Your *Buffalo News* covered our North American Bridge Championships in Buffalo. Because of my background in China and in business, my picture was in the paper. Many Chinese students, all of them Ph.D. candidates, came to visit. I was so delighted that I gifted them all with American Contract Bridge League memberships. They won three national novice championships. We started a pilot program in Buffalo because your newspaper covered us and the students came. We are going to fund Buffalo University for the first pilot program and it all came about because of your newspaper!

WB: I am going to tell you something interesting about that newspaper. We bought that newspaper in 1977. I never interfere with what they do editorially but I did notice the bridge column. The fellow who wrote the headlines over the bridge columns was giving away the nature of the hand... I told him to just put "Bridge by Sheinwold" instead of those revealing headlines. So they changed [the layout of] the bridge column. That was the only time I ever interfered with the newspaper.

... I don't know anyone who has ever played a reasonable amount of bridge who doesn't love the game. The problem is getting them to where they play that reasonable amount! I have a couple of friends I play with and we have a terrific time. I told them that if I ever play a hand really well, I want them to remember it and slowly play out the hand at my funeral service. As the pallbearers take me out they can say, "Boy, did he play that hand wonderfully." ...That's the perfect way to go.

Buffet's Revenge

The following hand was played on *OK Bridge*. Warren partnered with Sharon Osberg of San Francisco. Their opponents were Warren's sister, Bertie, and his brother-in-law, Hilton, who live in Carmel, California. Bertie and Warren have a close and loving but competitive relationship.

Warren viewed this hand as revenge. The previous time Warren and Sharon played them face-to-face in Omaha, Warren and Sharon "got killed."

"At that time," says Sharon, "Bertie tried to grab the score sheet for framing, but Warren stuffed it in his mouth and ate it!"

This deal was Warren's revenge:

North dealer, N/S vulnerable (subject to a greater penalty if they don't make their contract).

North (Sharon)
♠ A 5
♥ 7
♦ A J 10 8 5 2
♣ Q 9 6 3

West (Hilton)
♠ 10 8 4 2
♥ 6
♦ Q 9 7 6 3
♣ A 8 4

East (Bertie)
♠ J 9 6 3
♥ 10 8 4 3 2
♦ K
♣ J 7 2

South (Warren)
♠ K Q 7
♥ A K Q J 9 5
♦ 4
♣ K 10 5

The Bidding:

West	North	East	South
-	1♦	P	2♥
P	3♦	P	3♥
P	3N	P	4N
P	5♥	P	6♥

Opening lead: ♣A

Warren ended in six hearts and Hilton led the club ace followed by a second club. Warren won in hand and cashed two top trumps, learning about the bad split. He now cashed a club, led a diamond to the ace, and ruffed a diamond, as East discarded a spade. Next came the king of spades, a spade to the ace, and the queen of clubs. East was finished. If she ruffed, Warren would overruff, draw trumps, and claim. When she discarded her last spade, Warren did the same. Finally, a diamond was led and ruffed with the nine of hearts. Making 12 tricks. How about that—a trump coup executed by Buffet! Note that had he failed to cash his third club, the trump coup would have failed and the slam would be down one.

Malcolm Forbes: Motorcycles, Hot-Air Balloons, and Bridge

My interview with Malcolm Forbes took place in his office, which, in contrast with that of Warren Buffet, was lavishly appointed. Priceless artwork adorned his walls. Off in a cozy niche, a card and gaming table were ready to accommodate any visitor for a game of chess, backgammon or bridge. He welcomed me enthusiastically, as if we were already friends. As I scanned his office with my TV and camera crew, I acknowledged my good fortune: Bridge had given me access to 'the Boss.'

Our first few words concerned President George H.W. Bush, Deng Xiaoping, and the fact that this ever-challenging card game united all three men. Forbes expressed regret that he'd never gotten a chance to play with either leader, but added, with a wink, "I *did* get to meet Deng Xiaoping when I visited him in my hot air balloon, though!"

When I asked him for his philosophy on bridge, he told me, "Bridge is unique. You never pick up the same hand twice. It's good fun, a great way to relax, and the cost of playing bridge is almost nil—unless you're playing for money. But money isn't the point: the fun of the contest is what makes it exciting."

After the interview, we became great friends. At that time, I was organizing a Corporate America team to play against the already existing U.S. Congressional team. Laurence Tisch, then president of Columbia Broadcast System, was to be captain, and Malcolm accepted my invitation to play on the team.

Malcolm always liked to make a grand entrance. For the first Corporate America vs. U.S. Congress bridge match in Washington, DC, he arrived on the lawn of the tournament venue in his hot-air balloon. The press went wild, and the ensuing publicity guaranteed success for the various charities we were supporting.

The Corporate America team, with world-class player James Cayne (president of Bear Stearns) won by a small margin. Malcolm was hooked—he loved our method of competing, and he loved to win. Working with Patricia Cayne, James' wife, for the first Corporate vs. U.S. Congress bridge match, we decided to issue a challenge to the British Parliament team in London, in hopes of a three-way tournament. Sir Peter Emery, acting on behalf of the British team, accepted our challenge; moreover, his wife, Lady Emery, promised her cooperation as the tournament chairperson in London.

Our bridge tournaments were great successes. We raised money for charity here and abroad, and engendered good will among all the teams, despite the vicious competition. I invited Malcolm to go to London to play once again on the Corporate America team. He accepted with great excitement. "Kathie, how would you like to use my Old Battersea House as your tournament site?" I jumped at the chance and accepted his generous offer immediately. Though I warned him of the hordes of news media who might trample through his historic mansion, Malcolm brushed off my concern. "Call my assistant," he assured me, "she'll get you everything that you need."

This time Malcolm eschewed a hot air balloon for his corporate jet. He met the rest of the Corporate America Team in London: Larry Tisch, captain, Warren Buffett, George Gillespie III, partner in the law firm of Cravath, Swaine and Moore; Alan (Ace) Greenberg, chairman and CEO of Bear Stearns Company; Milton J. Petrie, chairman of Petrie Stores, and James E. Cayne, President of Bear Stearns and by far the best player on the team. To my great surprise, Malcolm was not one of the top three wealthiest men among these corporate players.

The British team was captained by Sir Peter Emery, and included the Duke of Atholl, Dr. John Marek, a Socialist MP, Cabinet member Lord Lever, Parliament's authority on international debt, and Lord Smith, President of the Royal College of Surgeons.

Malcolm's Old Battersea House was suffused with history. Designed by Sir Christopher Wren, it dates back to the 17th century. When Malcolm acquired the property, he installed many period art pieces, including a nod to Queen Victoria herself: a pair of her bloomers was slyly displayed in one of the washrooms on the second floor! The front lawn boasted a traditional English garden, behind which, incongruously, was a garage housing Malcolm's collection of Harley-Davidson motorcycles. An elegant spiral staircase greeted visitors, and I half expected Elizabeth Taylor to come gliding down those marble steps! I was overwhelmed by Malcolm's generosity.

At Malcolm Forbes' Battersea house for the CEOs vs Parliament bridge tournament, left, front, Laurence Tisch, center, Malcolm Forbes and Kathie.

Press releases and invitations were sent out. Security was very tight; Malcolm's security force and Sir Emery's security force combined to clear the press. Since Malcolm's name drew a lot of interest from the local and international press, having an invitation to the Old Battersea house was the hot ticket in town.

The Bridge Magicians

It was a classy and close match. Corporate America lost to the British Parliament team by a small margin, but the real winners were the press, who were all too happy to interview the rich and powerful in attendance. Audrey Grant, the well-known bridge expert, wrote in her article detailing the event: "Forbes' hospitality was unique. Although many of the guests had not met, he created an atmosphere that made the whole day seem like a family gathering."

At dinner that evening, in a more relaxed setting, Larry Tisch commented about his fellow teammates and opponents. "Because the bridge player becomes so engrossed, the mask slips and the real self is exposed."

Malcolm informed me that he had to fly home to New Jersey after dinner. The following morning, I received a phone call from Rixi Markus, the English grand dame and coach of the British Parliament team and my good friend. "Kathie, I have bad news for you. Malcolm arrived home and died of a heart attack in his bed shortly after." I was so shaken by the sudden and awful news. I notified his teammates, and with heavy and sad hearts, we attended his funeral at St. Bartholomew's Church in New York City. The church was filled to capacity. People had lined up around the block to pay their respects. A memorial booklet was printed for all of us. The cover read "While alive, he *lived.*"

Forbes Magazine paid tribute to my friend in an editorial entitled "Malcolm's last game."

The day before he died, Forbes told Kathie, "Bridge is one of the really great pleasures of life, on a par with motorcycling, ballooning, and writing editorials."

"His friends and admirers will be charmed to learn that Malcolm's last full day on earth was one of achievement and of delight to him... Just the day before he died he told Katherine Wei of the American Contract Bridge League: "Bridge is one of the really great pleasures of life, on a par with motorcycling, ballooning, and writing editorials."

It has been 30 years since Malcolm's passing. I still miss him, and treasure my friendship with the great man.

In 1991, a year after his death, the Corporate America team challenged the U.S. Congress again to play in "The Malcolm Forbes Tournament." His picture, along with my favorite quote from him, graced the cover of the American Contract Bridge League Bulletin.

> "If heaven is heaven,
> bridge must be there."
> —Malcolm Forbes, 1919–90

Deng Xiaoping: the Little Grandfather

Charles and I were at home one evening in 1981 when I received a phone call from the president of the Shanghai Bridge Association, Shen Jialing. To my great surprise, Mr. Shen invited me to come to Shanghai to help jumpstart their nascent bridge program, which was soon to hold its first international bridge tournament. I thanked him politely for the invitation, telling him I would consider and get back to him.

This honor, as I regarded it, gave me some cause for concern. The phone call had triggered the fear that if I returned to China, revenge would be exacted on me just because of my family's relationship with Chiang Kai-shek's government decades ago. Given the communist government's ongoing brutal suppression of opposition figures and voices, I viewed this as a real, possible danger.

I shared these concerns with Charles, reminding him that China's leader, Deng Xiaoping, was an avid bridge player. He nodded, smiling: not long before, we had met Deng, who was touring the U.S., at a Harlem Globetrotters exhibition game. Charles had contrived to slip one of his Precision books in English to one of Deng's aides, hoping that his book would be passed on to the leader. How happy he would be if a few million Chinese people, following their leader, would adapt to the Precision System! He encouraged me to go to China, assuring me that they wouldn't extend the invitation unless it was safe.

I called back Shen and accepted his invitation. Ultimately I became a cultural liaison who promoted friendship between China and the West. I have never regretted this choice.

I brought the first group of American bridge players to newly-opened China, Deng Xiaoping's formerly closed society. Our first stop en route to Beijing was Hong Kong, where Americans could learn about proper protocol and Chinese customs in an easier setting. Hong Kong was still under the democratic rule of England, and the setting of a five-star hotel was a much better classroom for me in which to educate my fellow travelers. These luxuries wouldn't be available to us in the Chinese communist society. Hong Kong's skyscrapers and worldly lifestyle were not to be found in China. I told everyone to put aside their capitalistic and western ways of thinking—to do otherwise would be perceived as insulting to our Chinese hosts.

In 1981, visitors to China had to bring personal items like medications, tissues, toilet paper, and other toiletries. Such articles were scarce, if non-existent, on the other side of the "Bamboo

At the invitation of President Jimmy Carter, Richard Nixon returned to the White House for the first time since 1974 when he resigned the presidency. The occasion was a state dinner honoring Chinese leader Deng Xiaoping. (UPI/Darryl Haikes)

Curtain." As our airplane began its descent at the Beijing airport, we saw a barren, grey landscape, dotted with insubstantial buildings. We were met at the gate by delegates of the Chinese Bridge Association and my youngest sister Joan. "Welcome American Bridge Players!" was displayed on bright red banners.

The Secretary General of the Chinese Bridge Association used his influence so that we were exempt from inspections at the customs gate. We claimed our luggage and got into a large bus. On the way to town, we saw many banners and painted slogans extolling the virtues of Mao and the revolution. It was clear that we were in a communist-controlled country.

Heedful of my warnings to lay aside their western judgments, our group gamely accepted their accommodations, a military guesthouse. Though not deserving of even one star, there was a benefit to staying in such a facility: we were able to see many things that tourists could not. Each morning, we watched military exercises and the changing of the guard. There were few cars, although thousands of bicyclists thronged the streets of the city.

Later in the morning, our guide came and took us to the Summer Palace. I remembered it fondly as the picnic spot place where Lao Chang brought us lamb sandwiches. The guide showed us Tiananmen Square, which was not well known in the West at the time, and memorials of Mao Zedong and Zhao En-Lai. The stone path we followed was flanked by imposing stone sculptures. We made our way to the palace terrace, where we were rewarded with a panoramic view of the city. Lunch was presented in the dining room of the Empress Dowager of the Qing Dynasty, and we absorbed the history as our hosts offered greetings and wishes of wellbeing.

Lunch and speeches concluded, the group met to continue their Beijing tour. At that moment I was discreetly—and firmly—pulled aside and directed to an imposing black limousine. Fearing an imminent arrest, I balked. My escort addressed me in hushed tones. "I am taking you to the Great Hall of the People to play bridge with Deng Xiaoping."

Deng was many things to many people. He was a political leader, the commander of the People's army, an architect of modern economic reform, a family man, a passionate bridge player, a victim of the Cultural Revolution, a hero to many Chinese, a bridge partner and personal friend—and a dictator.

Deng Xiaoping was born in 1904 into a large well-to-do family in Sichuan Province. Like many Chinese of his generation, Deng was a student of the Marxist-Leninist doctrine and studied in Russia. During the Chinese civil war, he fought alongside Mao and participated in the Long March fighting against the Chinese Nationalist government. Over the years, during his rise in power, Deng was purged multiple times. When Mao died in 1976, Deng, with the help of his supporters, returned to Beijing as a powerful leader. He called for rapid expansion of heavy industry, and for improvement in the sciences and education. He sought China's most academically talented to assist teaching the work force the skills necessary for economic modernization. He transformed China from the backward "weak man of Asia" into an upcoming economic superpower. By introducing capitalist ideas, Deng greatly improved the Chinese economy. However, many Congressional leaders in the U.S. blasted China's human rights position. They accused Deng's era of practicing "free-market Stalinism."

Deng's dictatorship appeared tyrannical to people around the world after the fateful Tiananmen Square massacre in June 1989. The uprising, and its horrific aftermath, made it clear that Deng couldn't accept democratic ideas. I was so conflicted. On one hand, I felt honored to have known him; nevertheless, I was dismayed that a man of his learning and foresight came to his own conclusions about democracy and freedom. It was not my place to criticize the old friend whom I had admired all those years, nor did I want to face the horror of admitting Deng's swift dispatch of the students in Tiananmen Square.

Two days after the massacre, I received a call from a *New York Times* reporter who asked if it was true that Deng was playing bridge while giving orders to shoot at the students.

Deng Xiaoping took up the game of bridge when he was a student in France in the 1920s. Bridge, though a card game, has the intellectual elements of chess. Understanding people and their personalities is crucial. The elements of psychology, logic, and competitiveness, suited Deng's own personality, and upon his ascendancy to power in China, he taught his staff, friends, and family how to play. During the Cultural Revolution, however, his playing was curtailed because Chairman Mao denounced bridge as a capitalist game, and antithetical to the values of the revolution.

After Deng was purged and later returned to power in 1976, one of his first reforms was to make bridge an official competitive sport as part of the All Sports Cultural Ministries. Deng encouraged the Chinese people to play, and in the Great Hall of the People, there was an exclusive 'bridge suite' set aside for Chinese officials.

In 1980, the president of the World Bridge Federation led a delegation to China. They formalized a deal that let the People's Republic of China into the organization, and that also allowed the Taiwan team to remain a member. I was overjoyed at the news. I had friends and relatives in both of the two Chinas. Now we could all play the game I loved— even at the same table.

My escort during my limousine ride brought me up to date: Deng Xiaoping, on hearing of my gold medal win in international bridge competition, wanted to meet a 'home-town hero.' He wanted me to assist in promoting bridge in China, and guide a Chinese team to victory on the world stage. You can say that this was the beginning of "bridge diplomacy" between China and the West. It was also the beginning of our decade-long bridge partnership—and friendship.

We approached the Great Hall and an imposing building, multiple city blocks long. This was where the National People's Congress, China's Parliament, convenes. We entered through large, polished brass doors and walked through what seemed like miles of hallways. We were ushered into the suite where Deng Xiaoping sat at a bridge table surrounded by men wearing Mao jackets. Deng rose and smiled at me as my escort made the introductions. He was a diminutive, sweet looking man; he could have been mistaken for somebody's grandfather. His appearance belied the immense power he wielded in China.

Our bridge foursome was formidable. We were playing with Wan Li, the onetime deputy mayor of Beijing, and Ding Guanggen, vice-secretary general of the People's Congress.

"What bidding system will we play?"

"Precision, of course!" answered my partner. He added, in a heavy Sichuan accent: "You are married to C.C. Wei. He gave me his Precision book and we are learning his system."

I nodded, smiling at the memory of the basketball game. Deng and I played Precision. Charles would be so happy!

Between hands, we chatted. Deng was friendly and seemed comfortable with me. He allowed me to call him by his first name, Xiaoping, and he treated me courteously. Deng was a chain-smoker; his teeth were stained yellow from years of smoking and drinking tea. When I asked him about his unusually short cigarettes, he replied, "My family cuts them short. They hope that this way I will smoke less."

We discussed his attraction to bridge. He explained that in his younger days, he patterned his military strategy on the tactics he learned and used at the bridge table. When he was purged, playing bridge was a good way to relax until his return to power. Now, "Bridge keeps my mind sharp." He was a fierce competitor who played to win, but not for money. His punishments for the losers? They had to crawl under a table! His partners would try to let him off the hook if he lost, but he was firm:

"It is the rule of the game," he'd respond.

After our bridge game, we continued talking for another two hours. Deng asked me to guide the Chinese national teams and to help develop and popularize the game in China. I responded with an offer to help the Chinese women's bridge team—the men would never take direction from a woman!

"I will be happy to help them learn Precision, so that they may compete at an international level. But first, they must learn to be able to read and speak English. As they enter the world stage, they will have to communicate with other players in English, the official language of bridge. They will need to study bridge books and train rigorously." Deng asked how long it would take to win medals at the world level. I considered my answer carefully before I replied. "I think they can win a medal in ten years."

In 1981, Deng was named "Personality of the Year" by the International Bridge Press Association for opening up the game of bridge to China. This was the first time a bridge award had been given to a world leader. I accepted the plaque on his behalf during the ceremony in Port Chester, N.Y., and delivered the award to him on my second visit to Beijing in 1983 when I began to coach the women's team. They were enthusiastic and diligent, and we continued our work when I brought them to the U.S. with the help of sponsors. In 1991, they won a bronze medal, and in 1996, a silver. Deng passed away in 1997, but not before his dream of a Chinese world championship was realized.

When Deng died, I was in Tel Aviv competing in their international bridge festival. Henry and I took a small bus to the Chinese Embassy to pay our respects. When we entered, we were asked to sign our names in the guest book. We bowed three times and said his name, according to Chinese tradition.

A little tact, a little creativity

In 1984, as Seattle hosted the Olympics, the World Bridge Federation, which was recognized by the International Olympic Committee, held its own competition. "Bridge for Peace" was the motto of the W.B.F. I was thrilled to be a part of this year's competition, for not only was the People's Republic of China going to be present, but also Ada and Ken had settled in Seattle.

Chinese Women's Team with Kathie, first row, second from the right.

I arrived a week early, to spend time with my children. Shortly after my arrival, however, I received a call from the 'leader' of the Chinese team. The leader, always a man, was in charge of both the men's and the women's teams' passports, money, and other important papers, and held them personally (so that no one on either team was tempted to run away) at all times. He was frantic. Their bus had made a rest stop, and someone had boarded the bus while it was empty and stolen the passports, the money, everything the leader was so carefully guarding! I calmed him, and assured him that I would take care of this problem. I paid for the bus, had them checked into their hotel, and called the Chinese consulate to re-issue passports for both teams. All seemed to be successfully resolved until, the day before the opening ceremonies, I received another call from Leader.

"Yang Lao-Shi ('teacher Yang' [my maiden name]), we cannot play in this tournament," the harried leader said nervously. He explained. Each member of all the competing bridge teams received a gift bag from the World Bridge Federation, which included pencils, programs, rules and souvenirs. Apparently the gift bags also included a small sticker, on which was printed "Made in the Republic of China"—*not* "The People's Republic of China."

"Let me take a look," I said, examining the guilty stickers. "No problem; I will take care of it right away." With that I called the wives of all of the presidents and other officers of the W.B.F., insisting that they come down and help with an urgent matter. Have I mentioned that I can be quite persuasive? Within a few hours I had all of the wives sitting on the ground, peeling off the little round discs that would have kept the Chinese team out of the competition.

There was one more obstacle, however, to a successful, peaceful tournament: the question of whether the Taiwan team would be permitted to play. At this time in history, the United Nations had kicked out Taiwan at the demand of the communist Chinese, who maintained that there was only one China. I had been the non-playing captain of the Taiwanese team in Rio de Janeiro, and wanted them to be a part of the Olympic tournament. It was important to me that both teams participate in this prestigious event. Bridge was another way for China to be a part of the world arena, and I wanted to see teams from my adopted country and my homeland sitting across from each other, competing. I called the captain of the Taiwanese team.

"Listen," I started, "I know you have pride—I have pride as well. This is the situation." I explained to him that The Peoples' Republic of China would never accept them as 'another' Chinese team. "But," I continued, " I think I have a solution that will allow you to stay in the tournament. Just call yourselves "Chinese Taipei." This might satisfy the PRC because it's only a place, not a country." In calling themselves "Chinese Taipei," which described the team without stripping them of any national pride, the PRC could not complain.

I continued. "I'm not for or against the Chinese. Legally, the W.B.F. has a right to kick you out, since there is only one China. But I am friendly with the head of the World Bridge Organization in Beijing. Let me see what I can do."

So in 1984, both the Peoples' Republic of China and Chinese Taipei had representation at the World Bridge Organization Olympics. Neither team medalled that year. It would not be until 2004, the year after I retired from bridge competition, that the Chinese women's team would win their first gold medal, in Philadelphia. However, both teams were able to enjoy the W.B.O. Olympiad and neither of them lost face. Diplomacy was my strong suit, but ingenuity was my 'ace in the hole.'

People along the Way

Shortly after I started playing bridge seriously, Charles took me to Washington DC. There was so much history there, but I was particularly taken with Arlington National Cemetery.

"Charles," I asked him, "Why are there so many cemeteries here?"

"Oh," he answered, "You are looking at the final resting places of national heroes."

"But what of all the *other* cemeteries around here?" I persisted.

Charles turned to me with a grin. "In *those* cemeteries are buried all the people who did not return their partners' lead in bridge!"

Bridge humor may not be appreciated by the uninitiated, but if you play bridge, you'd laugh—or at least smile—in recognition.

In my decades of dealings with bridge players, I have found that personalities can greatly affect the play of the game. Some of those who were pros at gamesmanship included the flamboyant Eli Culbertson, who boasted of the sexual connotations he attributed to bridge terms: *approach, forcing, one over one.* He made a special appeal to women that mastery of his 'system,' such as it was, would enable them to assert superiority over less well-instructed males.[13]

Early on in my bridge career, I was cautioned

that bridge was not a game for the female sex. I
approached the famous American player Oswald
Jacoby and asked him what it takes to become a
champion. Jacoby didn't hesitate.

"First," he said, "you have to be a man."

When we beat the Dallas Aces in 1978, I just
couldn't help it. After we had compared scores
and had won, I jumped and down and cried out:
"We won...we won!! We beat the Aces and I'M A
GIRL."

While competing at that tournament in New
Orleans, I had the opportunity to meet players from
all over the world, including the champion representing Egypt, Omar Sharif.

We teamed up with Benito Garazzo and Geor-
gio Belladonna, and along with Alan Truscott, the
noted *New York Times* bridge column writer, and
his wife, Dorothy, we toured Europe. In Ireland,
we noticed a throng of young girls lined up outside
the building where we were scheduled to compete.
Bridge fans? Not at all! *Funny Girl* had just been
released, and they were all there to get a glimpse of
the handsome leading man!

My teacher and partner, Benito Garozzo, sometimes had too much personality. Garozzo was a
passionate Italian who was prone to moodiness, and
when we competed, I had to take many precautions
to make sure his temperament would be suitable for
the bridge table. Before one tournament, I demanded his wallet. "Benito, you know how much you
love to gamble. When you lose, you are always in

1978 World Bridge Olympiad

Along with his successes in film—Lawrence of Arabia and Dr. Zhivago were international hits—Omar was an excellent bridge player.

a bad mood." He knew—he handed it over. I loved to tease him whenever I could. He was missing one finger on one of his hands, and I taunted him. "Oh, Benito! Did your partner cut it off for not leading his suit?" Fortunately for me—and for our team— he laughed.

World Champion Alan Sontag was on my Precision team. Once, before a tournament, I ran into him as he was sipping a glass of wine. I snatched the glass from his hand and poured it out. "Alan! Your drinking will affect our team!" I admonished. No wonder I was called the Dragon Lady.

Bridge can be like any sport. Tempers can run high and words can be uttered in anger, sometimes to the great embarrassment of the speaker. I was once asked if Barry Crane, an amazing bridge player and equally gifted director/producer (*Mission Impossible, Trapper John MD,* and *Dallas* were among his TV shows) could be on our team. We were competing for the prestigious McKenney trophy, but I was well aware of Crane's volatile personality. I was emphatic with my "No!" The rest of the team pleaded with me, and I finally relented. Crane was teamed with Jeff Meckstroth. Our team was up by a significant lead of 56 points in the first half, but eventually we lost the tournament. Barry was so upset with Jeff that he took their convention card, shredded it into tiny bits, and tossed it into his face.

"You'll never be a good bridge player!" he shouted viciously.

Jeff Meckstroth had the last laugh, though. He went on to become one of the top bridge players in the world.

Sometimes my bridge-playing friends just happened to be recognized for other accomplishments. It was not surprising to me that business titans like Buffet and Forbes played bridge: the game is all about strategy and getting inside an opponent's head. Another great player who ultimately became my close friend was the CEO of Bear Stearns, James Cayne, arguably the best player on our corporate team. When Jimmy wanted to expand to China, he asked me to be his consultant. Knowing of my experience in the shipping business and international diplomacy, he pressed me to open offices for him in Shanghai, Beijing, and Chunking. I was about to be married to Henry and start our honeymoon. I told him I couldn't.

Jimmy wouldn't be denied.

"What will it take for you to do it? I'll pay you anything!"

I gave him an exorbitant number, adding, "And I'd want two first-class airline tickets around the world when I'm done."

He granted my requests with no hesitation. I donated half the money to support the Chinese women's bridge team, and opened his offices. Those people really knew how to make money—and spend it.

When I wasn't competing in bridge tournaments, I was frequently raising money through the American Contract Bridge League for various charities. The ACBL knew they could count on me to get the big names for their fundraisers. At one national event, Sammy Davis Jr. was the guest of honor. Although short in stature, he was a giant among entertainers, and a gracious and compassionate man. I presented Mr. Davis with a check for $125,000 (a lot of money in 1964) to help in the prevention of child abuse, his number one priority. As the audience applauded his commitment, I whispered to him, "Look out there. What do you see?"

"I don't know," he whispered back. "What?"

"No one out there looks like you or me."

In 1985, I stopped in Chicago during the book tour for my first autobiography. I had been asked, as a bridge champion and best-selling author, if I would donate some of my time to help raise funds for the Chicago library. Of course I agreed. I was partnered with a young TV personality who was on her way up, but not as widely known as I. She was so warm and friendly—I knew she'd go far. All these many years later, I look at the photograph I took with Oprah Winfrey and smile. I like being right.

Kathie teamed up with Oprah Winfrey to raise money for the Chicago library.

Our charitable efforts supported first ladies in two administrations. I was honored to be a part of Nancy Reagan's "Just Say No to Drugs" project. Mrs. Reagan, a gracious and elegant lady, had welcomed Charles and me to the White House on a few occasions. We discussed her anti-drug campaign. I remembered my childhood experiences with Grandfather's opium dens and I knew how drugs could destroy individuals and families. We raised funds to help her achieve her goals, and did the same for another classy first lady, Barbara Bush. Her Literacy Project benefitted so many children, and I thought back to those two stately lions guarding the New York Public Library as the ACBL handed her a check in support of her foundation.

Success in bridge competition has been exhilarating and rewarding, and such fun.

Eight years after I won my first gold medal in international competition, Charles and I visited Taipei. President Chiang Ching-kuo, the son of Chiang Kai-shek, presented me with a special gold medal: a Chinese person had won a world event in bridge! He was so proud. A few years later I was named Ambassador of Bridge for the World Bridge Federation, and, as official adviser to the Chinese Bridge League, I became the only American to hold the rank of minister in China.

Afterword

My youngest granddaughter

Letter to my youngest granddaughter

February 21, 2021

Dear Katherine,

The 2021 Tokyo Summer Olympics starts to-night. I am so excited—I can't wait to see all those young people compete at the world level, and am happy that despite the ravages of COVID, the events are still taking place.

I know what it is like to compete at the world level; I can share the feelings of victory and defeat. Now you are competing as a young equestrienne, your mother watching proudly. Before leaving for your latest competition, you requested a picture of Charles—out of the blue—for good luck!

Katherine, Charles was the love of my life. The picture that I am sending you is from Larry and Debbie's wedding 40 years ago, and, placing it in the envelope to send you (I'm still not too great with email) I marvel at how quickly time moves, but how emotions and feelings never leave. I am grateful that you asked for the picture. You woke in me the joy and yes, the sadness that has come with my life with Charles.

You are a great kid, my youngest granddaugh-ter. Being *chosen* to be in a family carries its own special set of burdens and responsibilities, and you have made your parents proud-- you are bright, self-reliant, and accept the challenges of life with grace and enthusiasm. I am so honored to have you as my namesake, and I am proud of how Ava has raised you. (The fact that she gives me some credit for her child-rearing abilities has lessened, to some extent, my guilt for divorcing her father.)

I have lived an exciting life. With my father's help, I was able to come to America. I worked hard to become an American, but I couldn't accept just being a wife and mother. I wanted more. And so, for the rest of my life, with the help of those who believed in me and gave me their love and support, I worked to achieve my loftiest ambitions.

I have no regrets.

Your loving grandmother,

Kathie

Kathie is inducted into the American Contract Bridge
League Hall of Fame. Presenting the honor is
José Damiani, president emeritus
of the World Bridge Federation

Awards & Achievements

- 1985—President of the ACBL charity foundation, adviser to the A.C.B.L. Educational Foundation.
- 1986— Named "Bridge Personality of the Year" by the International Bridge Press Association.
- 1987—Named Ambassador of Bridge by the A.C.B.L. in recognition of efforts to promote bridge around the world, including bringing together China and Taiwan, and Israel and Egypt.

- 1989—Recognition for "enthusiasm, dedication and hard work in conceiving, organizing, and promoting the first annual U.S. Congress vs Corporate America Bridge Match."
- 1997/98—listed in Strathmore's Who's Who Registry of business leaders.
- 1999—Recipient of the prestigious Blackwood Award for service to the game outside of contributions as a player. (First woman to receive this honor.)
- 1999—Inducted into the Bridge Hall of Fame
- Official adviser to the Chinese Bridge League (Kathie is the only American to hold the rank of minister in China.)
- Grand Life Master in Bridge.
- Winner of four major world women's titles: The World Women's Pairs (1978), the Women's Olympiad (1984), the Venice Cup (1987), and the Monte Carlo Venice Cup (2003).
- North American titles include the Women's Knockout Teams, the Women's Board-a-Match Teams, and the North American Women's Swiss Teams.
- Non-playing team captain for 1971 Chinese team (silver medal) and 1991 U.S.A. Women's team (gold medal).

Acknowledgements

My heartfelt thanks to Henry Jacobson, who has spent countless months researching and compiling the facts that led to the first draft of this book, and for finding Meg Marsh, our much-needed editor, whose tireless and enthusiastic work has made my final dream book a reality. We have become fast friends, and her husband Donny and I have fun laughing at the same bridge jokes. Thanks to Bonnie Britt for her knowledge and expert assistance.

I would also like to thank Xiao Yu and her wonderful husband Dr. Michael Nadler, a perfect East-West happy mix. They saved my life when I broke my hip.

Finally, I want to thank my bridge children Lisa and David for sticking by me and playing Precision at all times!

Endnotes

1. American Bar Association, Transcript of Interview with Ada Shen-Jaffe, 2012 https://stacks.stanford.edu/file/druid:kp533js8274/kp533js8274_ShenJaffeA_Transcript.pdf, 8.

2. ABA, 3.

3. ABA, 3.

4. ABA, 3.

5. Charyn, Jerome, *Metropolis: New York As Myth, Marketplace, and Magical Land,* (New York:G.P. Putnam & Sons, 1986), 256.

6. Charyn, *Metropolis,* 257.

7. ABA, 7

8. *Congressional Record,* Vol. 133 No. 34, Washington, March 5, 1987.

9. American Bar Association, Transcript of interview with Ada Shen-Jaffe, 2012. https://stacks.stanford.edu/file/druid:kp533js8274/kp533js8274_ShenJaffeA_Transcript.pdf, p. 4.

10. Hollingshead, Daniel, "Mind Games," *ACBL Bridge Bulletin,* 75, no.3 (March 2009): 64

11. Sontag, Alan, *The Bridge Bum,* (New York: William Morrow, 1977), 202.

12. Truscott, Alan, *The New York Times,* May 26, 1969.

13. Mollo, Victor, *The Compleat Bridge Player,* (London: Methuen,1986), 132.

14. Michaels, James, "Malcolm's Last Game," *Forbes,* (April, 1990): 8.

Other books by Kathie Wei-Sender

Action for the Defense: when the enemy opens the bidding, Katherine Wei and Ron Andersen (New York: Monna Lisa Precision Corp., 1980), 245 pp.

"Defending Against Strong Club Openings," Katherine Wei, ed. Ron Andersen (Louisville, KY: Devyn Press, 1981), 9 pp. Championship bridge series, no. 7.

Precision's One Club Complete, Katherine Wei and Judi Radin, ed. (Monna Lisa, 1981), 169 pp.

Second Daughter: growing up in China, 1930–1949, Katherine Wei and Terry Quinn (Little, Brown, 1984), 243 pp.

On the Other Hand: a bridge from East to West, Martin Hoffman and Kathie Wei-Sender (Los Angeles: C&T Bridge Supplies, 1994), 135 pp.

Precision Today: your guide to learning the system—or fine-tuning your precision partnership, David Berkowitz and Brent Manley, ed. Kathie Wei-Sender (Memphis, TN: DBM Publications, 2002), 219 pp.

The Wei of Good Bridge, Kathie Wei-Sender and Martin Hoffman with David Burn (London: B. T. Batsford, 2003), 143 pp.

Made in United States
Orlando, FL
03 June 2022

18466564R00117